KINDFIDENT

RAISING OUR KIDS TO BE KIND + CONFIDENT

Written by

S. R. BRAUN

Tellwell Talent
www.tellwell.ca

ISBN
978-0-2288-0725-4 (Hardcover)
978-1-7737-0762-4 (Paperback)

♡

FOR MY PARENTS. THANK YOU.

CONTENTS

CONTENTS

PART ONE*

PART TWO**

* PART ONE has super awesome hybrid chapter names
** PART TWO has no super awesome hybrid chapter names but is still
worth reading

INTROCLAIMER

♡

INTROCLAIMER

....

INTRODUCTION + DISCLAIMER

First off, let me start by saying that I am completely unqualified to write this book. The idea popped into my head very suddenly while I was sitting in church one morning, and I spent the days following trying to convince myself that it was a terrible idea—that it wasn't so much an idea as a random thought that did not need to have any more attention paid to it. The very concept of writing a book on kindness seems arrogant because it implies that I am the kindest person in the world, which I am not claiming to be, as it seems that would be the type of individual that might be qualified to write on the topic. If that is the type of wisdom you were hoping for when you bought this book,* I apologize. Feel free to contact me, and I can give you some other titles written by much more qualified people such as Mother Theresa[1].

To make things worse, not only am I writing about being kind, I am also tackling the topic of confidence!

* That means not only did I actually finish writing this, it got published! And purchased! Sweet.

13

How smug! So now, not only am I arrogant, I have no struggles or insecurities at all. Ugh. Not true on either account. So, all this to reiterate—I am completely unqualified to write this book. In any case, I have some thoughts that I think are worth sharing. Qualified or not.

I went about the following week, dismissing thoughts of this book at increasing frequency, but the idea began morphing from just a word to pages and thoughts and ideas, swirling around my brain in alarming detail. As I could not seem to get the idea out of my head, I started to ask myself why I was against even considering writing a book. It came back to feeling unqualified. I am not an author. I am not a literary genius. I am a pretty good speller. I am a busy mom. I like to read but nothing earth shattering or overly profound*. I talk a lot but I also like being quiet and keeping my thoughts to myself. I have never had dreams or aspirations of writing a book. I barely remember the rules of essay writing from university. My outline for this book was literally scrawled on the back of a Costco receipt** while I sat in the car waiting to pick up my girls from school. I did teach one semester of Grade Twelve Creative Writing when I was twenty-two, so if any of my former students happen to read this book,*** I apologize if I haven't followed all the grammar rules I made you all follow. Like not starting

* I did read the entire Shopaholic² series in an impressively short amount of time.

** Seriously. Turn the page if you don't believe me.

*** Read? See first * on page 13

a sentence with "but." I am pretty sure I am going to do that at least once. But that's okay, right? Good, got that out of the way!

All of these initial reactions to the "book rejection" I was experiencing obviously gave me the resounding answer "no." However, I still couldn't shake it.

At this point, I hadn't mentioned it to anybody, not even my husband who I am usually incapable of not sharing everything with. Honestly, when I decided to actually tackle this project, my initial plan was to write the whole thing and attempt to have it published without anyone knowing. That way, if it was either rejected by the publisher(s) or I didn't even finish writing it in the first place, no one would ever know. Zero accountability—solid plan, right? And if I did actually finish writing it, and it did actually get published, I'd have all my Christmas presents taken care of, including an epic element of surprise!

"Oh, this? Yay, I wrote a book ... did I forget to mention that I was working on one? Oh well, Merry Christmas!"

So, all of this is to say: here I go ... very unqualified, slightly embarrassed* at even beginning to tackle such an undertaking, but I can't deny the force with which this idea has overcome me. So here we go. Thanks for joining me.

* The thought of someone peaking over the top on my MacBook and asking what I am doing makes me cringe. "Oh, not much ... just writing a book." Mental note: get some new awesome black frames and remember to straighten hair more often, just in case this scenario occurs. This will definitely improve my validity as an author.

Intro -
- not qualified
- Kind / co. = arrogant
- pride?
- suprise pub.
- A+Z ♡
- Kindfident
- contagune $≠☺
- Instascram
- nice sch lopper
- Averagephobic
- Country music $ MAMA BEAR ☺
- Words for your kids.
- Leader schmuck
- Private school thoughts
- Bullying (Bullstander)
- Brand name ≠ smug.
Houses, cars, etc.

PART ONE

KINDFIDENT

♡

KINDFIDENT

....

KIND + CONFIDENT

I love joining words together. It's fun, it saves time, and it makes ordinary moments feel like they are special and unique. Years ago, I was overly excited at a friend's engagement and I blurted out "Congragegagement!" which really is a much better way to say, "Congratulations on your Engagement." Honestly, it saves so much time—I can't quite believe there isn't a Hallmark Card that says this. Actually, I should probably trademark this before I attempt to publish this book. Don't try to steal this word—by the time you are reading this, I am pretty sure it will be trademarked. Anyway, now in our family whenever someone gets engaged it's "Congragegagement!" Try not to say it. I dare you.

Friday nights are one of our family's favourite nights of the week, and over the years, sushi and a movie has become our Friday night tradition with the girls. At some point, sushi and a movie became "Smooshi Night," and it was instantly even more fun and anticipated with its new, awesome name.

Bam. It's Smooshi Night! So much better.

The word "kindfident" has popped into my head off and on throughout the years. Over time, my "mom-friend group" has developed and grown and I can't imagine tackling this journey without them. Our conversations have developed along with our kids. From separation anxiety in primary school and scraped knees on the playground to sleepless nights worrying about the world our kids are growing up in after seeing something devastating on the nightly news. Every new school year brings an onslaught of new topics and, honestly, though our time together is always filled with hours of laughter, the parenting side of the conversations gets more intense and serious with every year that our kids get older. I guess this is normal as kids grow up, as they are exposed to more topics, different personalities and family values, more outside influences, the pressure of fashion, and society's obsession with beauty, social media, the list goes on and on. I must say—the primary school topics always seemed like they were a lot easier to solve. I think that is one thing I have had to come to terms with as a parent. We can't solve our kids' problems. It's easy to put a Band-Aid on a scraped knee, to sing a lullaby after a bad dream, to make that random Halloween costume your kid is determined to have*... but the problems that come along as our kids grow up can't be solved like that. I wish they could be.

But, as they grow up and learn to maneuver the currents of middle school—and thinking ahead to the culture of

* I am currently making a pickle costume for our youngest daughter...

22

high school—it is going to take a lot more than a Band-Aid or a pickle costume to make everything right in our kids' world.

But again, it's not our job to make everything "right." It's our job to walk alongside them and recognize the struggles they have and give them the skills they need to get through this crazy world as they get older. Not only get through it but also thrive and live well, with joy and passion and kindness and confidence. And here we go—segue to kindfidence.

Over the years, going back as early as Sunday school and Tot Soccer and kindergarten, believe it or not, the topic of girl drama has come up. Girl drama is inevitable. It has been around since the dawn of time. It will be around till the end of time. If you think you can avoid it, I'm sorry, you can't. No matter how many pink shirts we wear, how many conversations we have about inclusion and the damage cliques can do, it will always be rippling through the school environment. I personally do not think it does anyone's daughter(s) any favours to pretend that it doesn't exist. What we need to do is teach them how to navigate through these dramatic waters, when the climate of their friend group suddenly changes.

Girl drama is different than bullying. It can be trickier* in a way because it is, more often than not, actual friends who are the instigators—not some bully that you know you should avoid. We are taught to avoid bullies since before we can remember. It is a topic that is tackled head on—one of our earliest

---

* Please do not misunderstand this as being dismissive to how horrific bullying can be. More on this in Chapter 5: Bullstander.

lessons of socialization. Avoid The Bully. Recognize qualities of The Bully. Tell an adult if you are a victimized by The Bully. Learn skills to stand up to The Bully. It is instilled in us, and we in turn instill it in our kids.

But when do we learn to stand up to those forces in our lives that masquerade as our "friends?" The word frenemies* has floated around over the years, but it always seems to have an aura of humor around it. No one seems to address the wounds that frenemies can inflict. Stress suddenly begins to permeate things that used to be fun because somewhere along the way, the rules changed. Trying to navigate these things is a big deal. Trying to learn the rules on your own is nearly impossible. Mean Girls [3] was the go-to movie about frenemies when I was younger. I actually watched it again a couple of weeks ago on Netflix, and I can't lie—I had some pretty solid fits of laughter**. It amused me that this time around I identified more with the mom on the show, who tries desperately to be the "cool mom," so afraid to give her daughter any rules or boundaries.

Such a hilarious reminder to be confident when you are disciplining your children. A two-year-old having a temper tantrum may border on amusing, but that same behavior in a sixteen-year-old? Not cute. Not amusing. My parents have given me countless nuggets of wisdom throughout the years. One of my favourite tidbits of advice from my mom is when she told me to picture the actions of my toddlers as if they were teenagers. Try it. Seriously—everything

* I seriously wish I had come up with this word. It's so good.

** See Chapter 8: Parenting Philosofail. It is my "Get out of Jail Free" card for any part of this book you may want to judge me on.

24

will become clear very quickly when you trade in the pigtails for eyeliner, and the onesie for a crop top* and ankle boots. Those little behaviours are so easy to guide and mold and tweak (or, as my dad so perfectly calls it, pruning season) when they are small and lovely. Don't wait until your kids are older and the smallest bit of advice or gentle guidance is taken as a wager for all-out war. Okay, I will come back to more nuggets of wisdom later on in the book**.

Back to my tangent on girl drama. This topic seems to be coming up more frequently in our home as our girls get older. We have been fortunate so far to have only experienced minor girl drama but, regardless, a few things have started to become clear to me. For starters, don't assume your child is blameless—there are always two sides to the story. We are all guilty in one way or another. Whether you instigate it or silently support it, we have all either gossiped or accepted gossip about another person. More often than not, gossip has a role to play in girl drama. Secondly, all human social groups have a balance of personalities, with leaders and followers emerging among them. More than likely, it is someone in the leader role that instigates the girl drama and the rest of the group will be inclined to follow. This leader may be genuinely confident or she might be insecure and has learned to use her leadership role as a cover. So, try to look at the bigger picture. And finally, it is important to remember that just because someone has instigated girl drama, doesn't mean they are a

* For my girls: You will never be allowed to wear crop tops. Don't even think about it. Consider this your warning.

** See Chapter 17: Nuggets of Wisdom

write-off as a human being. We have all been involved in drama in one way or another. We all make mistakes and must remember that these are kids we are talking about. Kids whose brains haven't finished developing yet. So, when you are helping your child deal with these strong forces in their lives, give them the skills they need to stand up to the instigators and the confidence to not let the drama destroy their world. Sometimes the right answer is simply to let things go and try to have a thicker skin. This can be the toughest option of all but like it or not, this is a life skill we all need.

Though it may be true—and can definitely be a part of the conversation—simply telling your daughter that the Mean Girl is actually just insecure or jealous doesn't overly help them navigate the situation. You will need to acknowledge the bigger picture with your child. Help them understand how they can not only cope but also thrive when they are confronted with people like these in their lives. The thing about Mean Girls (I have two daughters, so naturally I gravitate to examples with girls—sorry to the parents of boys, they are a complete mystery to me. Perhaps try picking up a copy of Dr. Dobson's: Raising Boys [4]) is that they don't just exist in middle school or high school. The older I get, the more I realize that these personalities exist in the work place, the PTA, church, soccer club—the qualities (or lack thereof) that make people treat others badly exist within every level, every age, every demographic. So, let's teach our kids how to thrive and not just survive. Because it's not just middle school, it's life. Don't teach your kids to just "get through it" help them overcome it.

When you extract kindness from any human quality, you are left with a less than desirable outcome. Confidence without kindness leaves you with arrogance, a person overly fixated on their own self-importance. However, kindness without confidence leaves you vulnerable and timid, unable to handle the strong, destructive personalities of the overly confident, whether that confidence is false or not. But if you combine kindness with confidence you are creating unstoppable character in your child, boy or girl. When you are truly kind and have the confidence to act on it, to stand up to others, to be genuinely sure of your choices and know right from wrong, to accept yourself the way you are, it doesn't take long before these qualities shine out of us and have the potential to affect change that can truly make a difference in our schools and our communities.

I will wrap up this chapter with a simple multiple choice question for you. What combination of character traits would you want your child to have:

    a. Confidence - Kindness = Arrogance
    b. Kindness - Confidence = Timidity
    c. Kindness + Confidence = Unstoppable

Pssst...the correct answer is c)...just in case you weren't sure.

CONFAGANCE

♡

CONFAGANCE

··

CONFIDENCE + ARROGANCE

Yesterday was the first day my oldest daughter didn't hug me goodbye when I dropped her off at school. If someone had asked me ten years ago, when she was a bouncy, squishy baby, how I would feel about this milestone, I would have answered without hesitation, "devastated." Ten years ago, I was all that mattered to my child. I was her source of everything, as it should be during that particular phase of life. However, when I got back to the car and realized that this moment had occurred and passed so quickly, I was surprised to find that I did not feel even the least bit sad. The thing is, when these milestone events happen in life at the right time, you have to embrace them, celebrate them, and move on. Over the years, our school goodbyes have been rocky. There were never massive, out-of-control fits of crying, but seeing your child's big round eyes fill up with tears as they squeeze in as many extra hugs as possible before the final bell, well that can be even more gut- wrenching than a full-blown hysterical departure. But here is the thing—as parents, we can never lose sight of the fact that the goal here is to raise successful adults not happy children. And I firmly believe that if done properly, these two things don't have to be mutually exclusive. So, when I considered the end goal—a successful adult—as I watched my beautiful girl bounce into her grade six classroom that morning, full of joy and anticipation for all the fun the day would bring, calling excitedly to her friends as they reunited after a whole twelve hours apart, how could I possibly be sad?

I could have easily mentioned this moment to her after school, with a simple "Hey, sweetie, you forgot to hug me goodbye this morning!" At first thought this doesn't seem manipulative or selfish. But when you are raising a sensitive child, one that truly values family and cares about others' feelings, what is the point? If I had mentioned something to her, I would have made this moment about me instead of letting it pass by unmentioned, and I would have risked her feeling bad about the missed hug and set her development back instead of quietly celebrating her growing up in a natural and necessary way as she gained a new little milestone of independence along the way.

The core feature of this story is confidence. I want my children to be confident, as it really is a wonderful quality and is crucial to success and happiness. But the other trait involved is kindness, which is why I was intentional to not mention anything to my daughter. I know she would have cared—she is a deeply sensitive girl, but not in a volatile or emotional way, she just genuinely cares about other people's feelings. She did not reject me at school, she wasn't dismissive or rude—she was just happy as she confidently trotted off to join her peers and left me behind in a way that was perfectly healthy. If the departure had been rude and cold, if

I felt rejected or like I had, at last, reached the moment that I was an embarrassment* to her, that would be a whole other story. It is a subtle distinction, one that may not even be apparent to others, but such a crucial one to recognize. That is when you are treading in the muddied waters of confidence without kindness. When you remove kindness from a confident child, that is when arrogance creeps in. Segue into confagance.

Middle school is almost mythical in its ability to evoke fear in children and adults alike. This is where your son or daughter will suddenly morph from a lovely child to an unruly teenager that no longer likes anything about you.**

Side Note: One person now officially knows I am writing a book. My oldest daughter just peered over at my laptop and asked what I was doing. So, I did what any kind and wise mother would do ... I slammed my laptop shut and told her to mind her own business.*** Of course, that just intrigued her more as that is not my usual demeanor with her. After she proceeded to pester me with questions for the next five minutes or so, I finally gave up and told her I was writing a book. She paused a minute and then started laughing. Of course, my youngest daughter wanted to know what was funny— so now two people know.

* I have made both my girls pinky promise me that this will never happen, so I'm sorry but I won't be able to offer any wisdom on this.

** This was included in the above pinky promise.

*** I have not, and will not, claim to be perfect at any point in this book.

Oh, wait … she just shouted out "Hey, Daddy! Mommy is writing a book!" Three people. Sigh. There goes my awesome surprise Christmas present idea. Darn it.

End Side Note.

Okay—back to middle school. I admit it, I was apprehensive about leaving the warm, cozy security blanket of elementary school. The place with dancing flowers on the walls, where parents are welcomed with joy as children run into their open arms when the bell rings, where Band-Aids and lullabies can still fix everything. I had allowed the middle school stereotype to cloud my opinion of entering this new stage. However, my apprehension vanished almost entirely after the first parent orientation evening we had. Now, I think of myself as a very levelheaded person—I don't lie awake at night* worrying about things that are out of my control. I am not as carefree as I once was, which is normal as you grow up and become a wife and a mother, but I still would describe myself as a pretty easygoing person. But middle school. Yikes. That can rattle even the most chill of personalities. So, when I went to our first middle school orientation a bundle of nerves and left feeling not only calm about the years ahead but excited, I have to give credit to four points that the principal gave that evening:

* My husband will verify this—he finds it incredibly annoying how fast I fall asleep.

1. Your child will become a teenager in
   this building.
2. There is nothing you can do to stop it.
3. It's not their fault.
4. Try to enjoy it.

Seriously. How good is that? These four simple points have changed my attitude about the next phase of parenting. He went on to say that, as a principal, he thinks of himself as a tow truck driver. His job is to be there when the kids veer off the road and bring them out of the ditch, back on the straight and narrow, and then be there again when they veer off the next time.

This concept is so simple yet so profound. We need to be tow truck drivers to our kids. We need to give our kids the foundation they need, instill in them the values of family so they don't think rejecting parents and siblings is an acceptable stage of adolescence, and then we need to trust them. Trust them to go and spend their days well and as they get older, their evenings and weekends too. And be there when they need to be guided back to the right path. Tow trucks don't stay hitched to a functional car and take them to work or to the mall. When a car is working fine and no longer in trouble, it is unhooked and set free. But the tow truck will be there again the next time it has trouble. Not just one more time but as many times as it is needed, day or night.

My mom has always said that every stage of parenting was her favourite. This is easy to say but hard to show. Babies and toddlers seem easier than tweens and teenagers, but I think half the problem is that parents anticipate having problems with their teens.

And guess what? Kids are smart and they can tell when assumptions are being made of them. Don't assume the middle school years are going to suck. Assume they are going to be awesome. Your child will feel the difference, I guarantee it.*

I felt the joy of my mom's parenting. It was contagious. It trickled through our family and created this atmosphere that was amazing to be a part of. It brought us all together in a way that bred happiness and togetherness and left me filled up with a feeling of belonging. I always felt secure in my family identity.

I was a part of something—an invaluable member of a team that gave me an identity and a place where I belonged. My mom set the bar so high that I continually find myself comparing my parenting to hers. On the rare occasions** that I am impatient with my kids, I hear her voice and feel her patience and think, "Mom would have handled this better." The thing about high standards is you have to hold yourself to the same standards that you hold others. This is why my mom's standards were (and still are) inspiring instead of stifling. She was so consistent as a parent that I couldn't help but be filled with confidence about my place in the world. The environment you create in your home is the foundation for creating the right kind of confidence in your children. Feeling a sense of belonging and unconditional love, and being accepted in your own home is the cornerstone of healthy confidence. Add into that environment high standards for how you treat one

* I totally can't guarantee this, but I am pretty sure they will.

** See *** on page 33.

another, and genuinely have the same standards for your own interactions, and you have the secret to guarding and protecting your family against confagance finding its way into your home and into your children as they grow up.

NICESCHLOPPEN

♡

NICESCHLOPPEN

....

NICE + WASSCHLOPPEN*

When I was growing up, my Dad would always tell us, "Don't be a *waschlappen*." It was so much more effective than "Don't be a wimp." I immediately pictured a super lame, defeated- looking cartoon dishrag that I did not want to resemble whatsoever. Whenever he said that to me, I would instantly take a deep breath, square my shoulders, and find my backbone. Whether it was something going on at school, or my big brother teasing me relentlessly** my dad's go-to advice was "Don't be a *waschlappen*."

As I grew up, and eventually moved out on my own, got married, and became a mother, I still heard my dad's voice in my ear. This one funny German word has helped me to find my backbone in so many different scenarios throughout my life. Even though there was an unwavering expectation of kindness in our home, there was an equally unrelenting expectation that you knew how to stand up for yourself.

* *Waschlappen* is an amazing German word that means "washcloth." Pronounced "vushluppin." See page 47.

** You know you did.

Don't allow yourself be a victim, cowboy up, don't be a wimp—however you choose to phrase it, the message is the same. Stand up for yourself. Be confident. Walk tall, and look people in the eye. Know what you stand for. So when the time comes, you know how to stand up for these beliefs. So it becomes an intrinsic part of you. So when a situation occurs, you have an instinctive response to stand up for yourself, for others, and for what is right.

A common misconception behind wanting your children (and yourself) to be kind is that they simultaneously become wimps. That they can never disagree with someone, or get mad, or call someone out on their actions. But being kind does not mean that you have to be a *waschlappen*. It means that when a situation arises where you need to find your backbone, you will know how to handle things with integrity and intention. It means fighting the urge to say that perfect zinger that popped into your head, the one that would level your nemesis in one foul take down. We've all been there, pushed to the point of lashing out, and instead of the situation reaching a resolution, it escalates. What we need to do is make a choice in that split second and decide if we are going to be mean or kind. We can get our point across either way, but the way we choose to deliver it will either harm or help the situation.

Being kind does not mean being immune to all other human instincts. It simply means trying to make a choice to react in a way that honours ourselves and gets our message across without totaling our opponent. We've all heard the childhood rhyme a thousand times, "sticks and stones may break my bones but words will never hurt me." Not true. In fact it sends the message that our words have no ability to cause harm whatsoever, making us unaccountable to them. The truth is that physical wounds will heal but words can stay in our heads for ever. Words are powerful. Sometimes we need to use strong words to protect ourselves or others, but what we need to learn is how to take the "mean" out of them. We are not meant to be doormats. All of us, adults and children, need to learn how to stand up for ourselves. But we can learn to do this without putting others down in the process. That is where confidence needs to be inextricably linked to kindness. That is the point of this book. You can stop here if you want.*

I heard someone say once (I wish I could remember who it was so I could add a tiny number beside this and give them credit at the back of the book) "You can disagree completely with someone, on every topic, and still be kind about it." This uncredited quote nailed it. It's not about agreeing with everyone, nodding your head listlessly and always walking on eggshells so you are never the cause of any conflict. It is about knowing who you are, what you stand for, and how to live that unapologetically.

Our homes all have their own unique climate and vibe. It's a huge part of what makes a family original. Some of these things we can control, some we can't, but each intricate part of our families shape the climate in our home. A family that has four boys, for example, is naturally going to have a different vibe than a home with one girl. Single parents naturally have a different atmosphere in their home than one with two parents. But whatever the "structure" of your family, you can make it work in a healthy way. My brother is a single dad of two little girls, and he has

* Please don't.

43

intentionally created an atmosphere in his home where his personality and interests have shaped his girls' activities and how they spend their time, so they can really know him as a person* as well as a dad. This is so important to remember. Being a parent is not supposed to make you a robot that packs school lunches, gives chores, and nags kids to clean their rooms. Your kids need and deserve to see the real you, the person not just the parent. It helps them understand themselves and where they came from. Show your kids your personality and humor and quirks. Share your interests with them and allow them to have their own interests they can share back. This doesn't mean we are "peerenting,"** or becoming their buddy, we are still the authority figure, but we can be our own versions of that. You are your child's perfect parent. You are the only one they know, the only one they get, so be your best version of it.

Growing up with a big brother, I was exposed to a wider variety of activities than we have in our home now. Part of this is having two girls, part of it is their unique personalities and the interests that they have. But growing up with my brother, I was exposed to a variety of things like Scouts, snowmobiling, canoeing and of course Star Wars—along with the daily teasing that comes with being a little sister. All of these things merged with my interests and hobbies, along with my parents', and created our unique family vibe. One thing in particular that merging of family interests

* Not gonna lie—a lot of this is based around Star Wars and Harry Potter.

**Thank you Phil Dunphy[5]

creates is tolerance. I learned to tolerate, and eventually appreciate, Star Wars. The same cannot be said for Star Trek. My brother learned to appreciate and enjoy horses and making beaded earrings.*

One of the main things I appreciated learning from my big brother was how to take a joke. This is one area that we are failing our girls on. I know it seems unimportant, but there is a huge gray area where girls are given a free pass to act like … oops, I can't say that … act like drama queens. I have seen so many girls turn into complete emotional disasters in a split second when someone dared to tease them. I am not talking about cruel teasing—I am talking about normal family teasing. People have been treating girls like they are glass objects that can't handle any disruption to their fragile beings. It goes something like this:

1. Dad/brother/uncle hanging out with sister/daughter/niece.
2. All is well.
3. Dad/brother/uncle makes a joke and/or teases sister/daughter/niece.
4. Emotional hell breaks out.
5. Girl is given free pass.

This is wrong on so many levels. Girls should not be given a free pass because of their emotions. You are training your daughter to be psychotic in puberty if you let her get

* No, he didn't. He once told me that my beaded earring obsession was boring, and he was glad he wasn't my friend so he didn't have to do it. Not nice bro. Not nice at all. Kinda true, but that is beside the point.

away with these "free passes" when she is younger. Being kind is a standard for every day, every gender, every mood—hormones are no exception.

My girls don't have a big brother, but rest assured, my husband has stepped up to the plate. He has made it his personal mission that our girls can handle being teased. The other day, while driving in the car, we were audacious enough to put on a song that my husband and I liked. Not "Let it Go." Nothing from *Moana*. No Disney princess vocals involved. I know—the nerve, right? Our girls, predictably, reacted strongly to this offence to their ears. Honestly, if it was just me in the car I probably would have skipped through to the next song, but my husband? Nope. He turned the volume up, hit "repeat" and settled in for the long haul. There were moments of ugly shrieking from the back seat, but the volume button just keep going up with each protest. Eventually, they gave up. The song wasn't changed until there was submission from the back. Well done, sir. Well done.

He also loves to wake them up for family vacations like in *Home Alone*. The house will be quiet and cozy, bags packed and waiting ... and there he goes— running into their rooms, turning the lights on and shouting, "Get up!!! We slept in!!! We are going to miss our flight!" The first time he attempted this, I held him back, trying to avoid the meltdown I was sure would happen. But guess what? They woke up, startled for sure, but within seconds were in fits of uncontrollable laughter. Not the way I would have started our vacation, but there are two of us parenting these kids and we both need to add our own styles to the mix.

As much as we don't want our children to
be *waschlappens*, we can't let ourselves become
Momschlappens and Dadschlappens. That is why we
need to bring our own personalities into the mixture.
Let your kids see the real you. Show them who you
are, what you like to do for fun, what music you like to
listen to. Stand up to them when they are being rude
to you. Don't be a wimp. Have a backbone. Cowboy up.
You are all an important part of your family, so don't
let your kids call all the shots. Don't be a *waschlappen*.

WASCHLAPPEN

LEADERSCHMUCK

♡

LEADERSCHMUCK

....

LEADER + SCHMUCK

It is said that there are leaders and there are bosses. A key difference is that leaders show you what to do and bosses tell you what to do. There is more to it, obviously, but that is a simple way of explaining the difference. Bosses inspire fear, and leaders earn respect. Bosses place blame, and leaders accept blame and resolve problems. There are dozens of examples, but the core feature of this type of boss is confagance. If you dozed off in the last chapter, I will recap it for you: confagance is confidence and arrogance. When someone in a position of power lacks kindness, you have a dictator—someone who cares for themselves, but not for those under them. Whether it is the head of the school council, or the CEO of a huge corporation, if there is a leader without compassion or kindness he or she will inevitably be a schmuck. A leaderschmuck. It is a leader without any of the good traits. It's a bosshole. Someone on a power trip. We all know someone like this. It is someone who cares about their position of power, however big or small, more than the good of the people under them.

So how does someone become this way? How do people get in positions of authority and leadership without caring for those under them? It is not a simple question and, like most things in life, there is not a simple answer. But we can try to deconstruct examples of failed leadership in our world and attempt to identify some of the missing factors.

Being a kind and benevolent leader does not arise from just one dominant trait or characteristic. Layers of building blocks come together to create this type of individual. Building blocks that consist of selflessness, confidence, compassion, awareness of others' needs, kindness, wisdom, and intelligence ... it is a perfect storm of traits. This type of person needs to be driven, with a strong desire to succeed in whatever endeavor they undertake, whether it be entrepreneurial or political or otherwise. This person could be a sixty-year-old politician or an eight-year-old crushing it with a neighbourhood lemonade stand. The world is full of kind and wise leaders that have made a positive impact on a large or small scale. Some have gone down in history, and some we have never even heard of. But the names you are more likely to recognize are those leaders that have gone awry. The ones that lost their way or never had their feet on an honourable path to begin with. So, what is missing within these people, and what can we instill in this generation of youth to safeguard against creating more misguided leaders?

When too much focus is placed upon the importance of a child as an individual, allowing them to forget about their role within the greater community and world, narcissism starts to creep in. *Psychology Today*[6] defines a narcissist as someone exhibiting "grandiosity, a lack of empathy for other people, and a need for admiration.

People with this condition are frequently described as arrogant, self-centered, manipulative, and demanding."

Though narcissism is not new to this generation, it is definitely on the rise, and our culture of selfies and social media exacerbates this abnormal focus on the individual rather than on the larger picture. It is possible to start to counterbalance this selfishness with simple things like volunteering in your community, donating to local charities, or contributing to the million other areas of need in our world. Every single decision you make, big or small, will shift your child's focus off of themselves and towards others. We need to make a concerted effort to tip the focus away from ourselves. Find a balance that works for your family and start small so that it is an enjoyable experience. No one, including myself, is going to be overjoyed if they are suddenly forced to donate all of their belongings to the needy and spend all of their free time picking up litter. So be sensitive to the process of change. Every single minute that is spent focusing on someone or something other than yourself is a win. If it is five minutes a week, that is five minutes your teenager isn't on Instagram. Win.

The hope is that by consistently fostering these traits in our children, they will grow up with these characteristics becoming intrinsic. That is when we will see young adults emerging as kind and confident leaders and bosses that remember the needs of those under them instead of being caught up with their own self-importance.

It will be a slow process but we need to collectively begin to counterbalance the importance of the individual in our society. I used the stereotypical example of the teenager on Instagram, but let's be serious—it is every age and stage that is staring down at their phones, disengaged from everything that is going on around them. It's me, too—I am not absolving myself from this trend towards selfishness. I don't spend nearly enough time thinking of others, giving to those in need, or looking up from my own self-made universe. There is nothing in this book that is meant to put myself on a pedestal. It is not meant to be preachy or smug. I do not have it all figured out, my kids are not perfect,* and I often find myself thinking of "me" rather than "we." It is a journey. And I am on it too.

But I think we can all agree on a need for change. And why wouldn't we want to try and make the generations to come care more about this world and the people in it? Let's teach our kids to look up from their phones long enough to see what is going on around them before it is too late. Teach them to invest in things that matter, to notice the needs of others, to take action where there is inaction. It is a beautiful world that we live in, but we need to raise future leaders who will care for the people and the environment around us so that it stays beautiful for as long as possible.

So, let's start small. It is as simple as not letting your toddler boss around all the other kids at a play-date. Making them share and take turns. These are simple things that are fairly easy** to change at this young, formative age. It's making your kids help out around the house without getting compensated or overpraised. It's encouraging your teenager to get involved in their school and their community. It's helping your kids find things that they are passionate

* Sorry girls :)

** Easy-ish

about and supporting their interests and hobbies so that they aren't spending all of their time thinking about themselves, what they look like, and how many likes they get on a post. It's making them look upward and outward, away from themselves.

These changes may seem small, but they start the trend towards thinking of others and caring for things and those outside of themselves. This is what is missing in so many of the leaders in our communities. Remember that a lot of little things add up to something big. So, let's start small and see what we can do.

BULLSTANDER

♡

BULLSTANDER

....

BULLY + BYSTANDER

Bullies. They have been around since the dawn of time. And, sadly, they will probably be around until the end of time. Out of all the chapters in this book, this is the one I have been most hesitant to write. In fact, I skipped it altogether, left it blank and went on to finish the rest of the book first. It is easy to be light and silly with so many issues in the world of parenting and families, and having a sense of humour really does help with so many things. But not with bullying.

There is nothing funny about this horrible epidemic that seems to be sweeping our schools and communities. And the world of social media seems to aggravate this already toxic problem. There has never been a higher rate of teen suicide in our nation, and more often than not it seems to be linked to some form of bullying.

The root cause of bullying is too big of a topic for me to tackle—for that, I truly am unqualified. There are so many factors involved in what makes one person bully another, ranging from abuse in their own home that makes them lash out at others, to simply having been over-indulged in their own self-importance and place in the world, resulting in a warped sense of power, thinking they have the right to control another's happiness and destiny.

I have touched on a few reasons that can increase one's susceptibility to becoming a victim—the key ingredient being the lack of confidence that is pervasive in this generation of youth. Obviously it is never someone's fault that they are a victim, which goes without saying, but we can do our best to give our children the tools they need to try and combat this potential danger in their lives.

But rather than focusing on the bully and the victim, the two key forces in this equation, I would like to look at an equally troubling factor that often gets overlooked: the bystander. The person that isn't directly involved but has the potential to intervene and affect change, should they choose to. I don't know if we will ever be able to eliminate the presence of bullies in our world and, consequently, the victims they target, but I do hold out hope that if we could target the rest of the equation—the bystanders—we could make a real difference. People are inherently follow-ers. That is why those with strong leadership skills stand out and have the ability to lead others. If these leadership skills are good and true with pure intentions, then they hold the power to create change in a wonderful way. Of course, if these strong leadership traits are founded on less than honourable intentions, well, we have seen throughout history the horrors that this can bring about. But if we could target and empower the larger population and teach them to stand up to these forces, to identify these negative influences and know how to avoid them, it would be a step in the right direction.

We don't necessarily think of bullies as leaders—they aren't usually granted a title that could be linked to a positive trait. But the truth is they do inherit some leadership qualities, otherwise they wouldn't have the confidence (authentic or otherwise) to dominant others. And there is almost always a group of followers that support this leader—the bully—for some reason. Whether it is a conscious decision based on wanting to participate in cruelty, or a subconscious way of protecting themselves from ending up as the victim, a bully almost always has a support group. The members of this entourage are the ones encouraging the behaviour, though not necessarily taking direct action themselves. But their inaction is still endorsing cruelty, and what we need to do is connect with these individuals in a way that will empower them to stand up to the bully. We need to develop their conscience so they know there is a line that needs to be drawn and give them the confidence to speak up when that line is being crossed.

The typical victim doesn't necessarily always have a "group." They often keep to themselves and exhibit classic introverted traits, lacking the traditional leadership skills that make someone able to stand up for themselves. This makes it even more essential that we somehow reach the bystanders, so they have the awareness and confidence to stand up for others, regardless of whether they are friends or not—simply based on the fact that we are all human and deserve to be treated kindly.

The bystander is the everyday kid. The kid that doesn't stand out as a loner or a leader, but the kid that is happy and friendly and well adjusted for the most part. The kid that isn't targeted as a victim and doesn't present as a bully. This is the type of person we need to empower. Encourage them to use their voice so they can speak up in defense of those who can't speak up for themselves.

This isn't something that happens overnight, but if we can slowly start building up our kids with these qualities and speaking into their lives to bring an aware-ness of the need to stand up for others—it is a huge step in the right direction.

Since I have been writing this book, the movie *Wonder*[7] has been released and taken the world by storm. Our world anyway. My daughter's class is currently reading it as their grade six book study. Both my girls have read and re-read both *Wonder* and *Auggie & Me*,[8] and it is always the number- one request for movie night. If I could give this book a standing ovation, I would. I could not imagine a book or movie that has more potential to inspire change in our kids than this one.

The author, R.J. Palacio, has written such endearing and relatable characters, you are certain to identify with at least one of them. She walks the reader through the mind of the bully, the victim, and the bystander in a way that is so authentic and relevant that kids are able to see themselves clearly within the world that she creates. She takes you on a journey of self-discovery from the perspec-tive of each of these characters—with the victim finding the quiet confidence he needs to survive and thrive in his first year of middle school, the bystander finding his own resolve and convictions to be the voice that stands up to the bully, and the bully experiencing sincere regret over his actions—with a brilliant glimpse into the parental influence that caused his callousness in the first place. Reading this book, and watching the movie with my kids, first in the theatre and then multiple times at home, coined a new phrase in our house: The Mom-Cry*.

* This in no way lets Dads off the hook. The Dad-Cry is real. How else do they always know the exact right moment to pass you a Kleenex?

I am not one that cries easily in "real life" but put on a country song, give me a sappy card, or show me a movie about animals and I am weeping.

So, if you have seen *Wonder,* you can imagine the amount of Kleenex I went through. And my girls, as much as they loved the movie, totally don't get why I get so teary-eyed over it. The best way I could explain it was simply that it was a Mom-Cry kind of movie. You just can't get the full range of emotions from it if you aren't a mom. So as I have Mom-Cried my way through the book and the movie, I have thought a lot about the characters and keep coming back to the role that the bystander played. He struggled along the way but eventually was such a crucial part of the bully's journey to find remorse over his actions. He eventually found the courage and the voice to be more than an observer to the cruelty he saw and inspired his peers to do the same.

Two of the best phrases in the book are: "Be kinder than necessary" and "Choose Kind." This is what we need to be modeling and teaching our kids. This is how we can empower the bystander to be compassionate and protective of the victim and how to stand up to the bully.

So give it a try—be kinder than necessary. Make this the expectation for your kids. Not the bare minimum of kindness, but above and beyond what is expected. "Choose Kind" and see the change start to trickle through your family, your neighbourhood and your school. We have to start somewhere, so start with this and let's see where it takes us.

Ok, that's it for now. I'm going to go order some Indian food and watch *Wonder* with my kids. And Mom-Cry, of course.

INSTASCAM

♡

INSTASCAM

···

INSTAGRAM + SCAM

I actually love Instagram, even though the name of this chapter would suggest otherwise. I am not, by any stretch, addicted to social media, but I really do enjoy scrolling through and looking at pictures of my friends' kids on their first day of school, seeing their Halloween costumes and, of course, the Christmas morning pictures with just the right filter so the lights look extra cozy. And I, in turn, enjoy posting these highlights as well. The important thing to remember is that is exactly what these are. Highlights. These are the bright and shiny moments that people choose to artificially represent their life. I recently heard of a couple I know that were getting a divorce, and my first thought was that they seemed so happy on Instagram. I went back and scrolled through their pictures and almost right up until they announced their separation, their Instagram feed was filled with happy moments and matching hashtags* to go along with them. And that is the trouble with Instagram. You have complete control of the window through which the

* #blessed #happyfamily #lovemyhusband #yougetthepoint

world sees you. All the moments can be perfect and can be presently perfectly, and even if they aren't perfect, they are adorably imperfect. With this ultimate control comes a complete absence of authenticity and vulnerability. Now I am by no means suggesting that we should all post our most raw, messy moments, we are allowed to pick and choose. I am simply warning you not to compare yourself and your life to what is going on in your Instagram feed. There is nothing more irritating than managing to barely get through a busy school morning after hitting snooze three* times, skipping your shower, throwing cash in the kids' lunch bags because there is no time to pack a lunch and grabbing a bagel at a drive-thru on the way to morning drop-off which you barely make it to** before the last warning bell… and then, when you finally make it back to your car before heading to work, you sink into the driver's seat, grab onto your two precious moments of "me" time, and pick up your phone to check Instagram…

<< Insert picture of a shiny, happy, showered, well-groomed and relaxed mother here. >>

"Sunrise yoga was amazing this morning and the kids loved their organic breakfast buffet and this vegan smoothie is just what I needed before heading off to volunteer at the animal shelter #sleepisfortheweak #coffeenotneeded #skippingyourshowerisgross #drivethrubreakfastbagelsareforfailures"

* Six.

** No, you don't.

Okay, before you do anything drastic you need to know one thing: You just got Instascammed. That picture you just saw? Not taken right after a workout. The organic breakfast buffet? Her kids had Pop-Tarts. Animal shelter? Nope—she's going for Botox.

Don't allow yourself to get caught up in the destructive cycle of social media competition. It is important that you realize I am not telling you to delete your apps and never look at your phones again—quite the opposite. I am telling you to take it all with a grain of salt. Our new world is driven by technology and social media. It's weird, but it's true. So you need to figure out how to have a healthy relationship with it, not just for yourself but so that you can authentically model this to your children. In the same way that we don't want our kids to "get through" middle school because they need to learn how to handle it in order to truly succeed—they also need to learn how to handle technology and social media. So who is their primary example? You may think that their peers are, but I believe a more accurate answer is their mother and father. It's you. The difference is they may not talk to you about it, but they watch you and your spouse and how you handle your free time. If you have a phone in your hand at the dinner table, then you have no leg to stand on if you tell your teenager to put theirs away. The quickest way to lose respect with your kids is to be a hypocrite. It's a strong word when it is only a phone we are talking about, but I believe phones have the ability to destroy family relationships. Or at least cause significant structural damage. Again, I am not suggesting to ban them—that will backfire, I promise you*—but model

* Obviously I can't promise this but if I am wrong, well done!

appropriate phone use and that will be your best way to ensure your child respects you when you ask him or her to put their phone away.

If you pick up your phone every free second to quickly check your Instagram feed or whatever your go-to platform is, you are training your kids to disengage with you. If you post every moment of your life, you are modeling that your self-worth comes from how many "likes" you get throughout the day. You are also teaching your children that there are no private moments that are to be cherished just as a family. This inadvertently devalues family time. If you share your most precious, intimate moments with all of your "followers," they are instantly no longer a precious, intimate moment.

Don't teach your children that their value comes from their interaction on social media. Teach them that their value comes from their place in your family, and their identity comes from who they are on the inside, their talents and interests and humor and quirks—the real things that make them who they are, that make them unique and special. The idea that self-worth has anything to do with a device is absolutely ludicrous. However, these devices will be a part of our kids' lives, so it is our job to teach them how to use them properly. If you ban phones from your teenagers, the minute they move out they will be overdosing on social media without having learned how to use it in a healthy, non-destructive way. Let them figure out the truth and lies that social media tell us in a safe environment that allows you to help them learn where their true value comes from—and it's not from something they can hold in the palm of their hand. Don't let your kids get Instascammed into believing otherwise. If they see you comparing your life to what you see online and that it makes you feel unfulfilled, you can be sure that they are learning to compare themselves to what they see online. In the same way that mean girls will appear in every stage of life so you better learn to deal with them, your kids have to learn how to deal with social media. Because it doesn't go away, it just presents itself in different ways with different topics. The teenage girl sees dozens of different images of beauty and size-zero models and has to learn that they have been altered and not to compare herself to them. The teenage boy needs to learn to protect himself from the overwhelming onslaught of sexual imagery available to him online, so that when he is a husband and father he won't be vulnerable to these images. The new mom needs to not compare her body to the other moms online that seem impossibly fit. Every person, in every stage of life, has to learn not to value themselves by what they see online.

It doesn't stop after you are an adult. As hard as it is for teenagers to not get caught up in the comparative cycle of social media, moms have it almost as bad, if not worse. Have you seen some of these Pinterest birthday parties? And how some peoples' houses look?! The level of perfection is staggering. Literally one glance at some of these posts and you instantly feel insufficient as a wife and mother. My cake pops have never, ever turned out like they look on Pinterest. And I was an Art Major! Seriously, how do the Math Major moms' cake pops turn out?! So don't compare your kid's birthday party to a professional decorator that knocked it out of the park. More than likely that post was part of their job and not just a candid shot of perfection. There is absolutely nothing wrong with this and is actually pretty cool that there is a new booming industry for moms that have a knack for design and fashion—but it doesn't mean that your party wasn't awesome too. My husband and I work together and there is a large component of our company that really benefits from social media and the illusion of perfection. I have styled more than one scene that depicts perfection, and there is nothing wrong with this. Just don't forget that it isn't real. Sure, the products are real, but they did not spontaneously appear in the quaint and delightful way that the people on the other side of their phones see them. Some of my favorite sites to follow on Instagram are the designers and moms-turned bloggers that showcase their lives and homes and children in adorably perfect ways, with great decor and healthy, beautiful food. I have gotten a lot of great ideas over the years from sites like this, but I don't expect my everyday life to mirror theirs. Comparison is where the unrealistic expectations come into play and the inevitable feelings of failure or disappointment follow.

Remember that if your child sees you constantly comparing yourself and your achievements to what other people have posted, you are teaching them to compare themselves, too, to a level of perfection that isn't real. Or necessary, for that matter. So if your house decor isn't quite as perfect as the home decor sites you follow, oh well. If it bothers you that much, stop following those sites. If your cake pops suck, that doesn't mean the birthday party was a failure. Post the picture anyway. Or don't. That's the point—don't let social media make the rules—you make your own rules and decisions about what is awesome and what isn't. Don't let Instagram decide if you (or your kids) are awesome or not—that is a power that it doesn't deserve and should not hold.

AVERAGEAPHOBIC

♡

AVERAGEAPHOBIC

....

AVERAGE + PHOBIC

I will never forget the first report card that our daughter got. It symbolized the beginning of a new era of parenting. Gone were the long days that you could fill how you want. No more pajama days, going to the zoo on a Wednesday, having a pancake brunch on a Monday. It was the beginning of alarm clocks, school lunches, drop-offs and pickups and homework. The start of school brings a whole new world and with it, the start of your child being compared with others. It may even happen a little bit before school: whose baby walks first, who says their first word sooner, but when school starts, it is official. Literally official—you get a report on how your child compares with others.

So the first report card is a big deal. How does my little wonder child fit in with the rest of the class? I held the envelope in my hands and nervously tore open the flap. I looked at it, blinked a couple of times and handed it to my husband. Staring at it together, we saw the middle row dominated with marks. Nothing in the best column, nothing in the worst, but the middle was chalk full of marks. Our child was a Middle Row champ. Not horrible, not excellent. Just middle of the row. My parents were over that particular day and I held the report card up and announced grandly (not in front of my daughter of course) "I am proud to announce that we have an exceptionally average child!" My dad has never been one to offer unsolicited advice, but he said something to me that day that I will never forget. He simply said, "Everyone is so afraid to have an average child, but people have forgotten that average kids usually make the most successful adults."

Wow. Talk about a game changer. With this one simple sentence he stripped away all the foolishness that we put on our children. Parents have become obsessed with having an "excellent" child. It has become normal to ask, "what does your child do?" instead of "how is your child doing?" Parents begin competing in the art of child excellence when their kids are only a couple of years old. Whether it is sports or academics or music, kids' programs have started recruiting younger and younger children. Two-year- olds that can barely walk are wobbling around on skates, toddlers are learning to play the violin. Preschool-age kids are filling the rooms of Math Enrichment centers. There is absolutely nothing wrong with your child being involved with extracurricular activities, in fact, they should have good, healthy things that they enjoy doing to fill their time with as they get older. It is a wonderful use of time. But when kids are getting groomed to be the next big ticket item in whatever activity their parents have chosen for them, the balance gets lost and you start to lose the well-rounded child. The percentage of kids that actually go on the be a professional hockey player, musician, or actor is so small that if they don't attain it, many of these youths have no identity outside of their chosen activity.

If you do choose to streamline your child's activities in hopes that they will be the next big thing, you have to be extra intentional that they have an identity outside of this activity as well. There is an expiration date on almost all great skills, so if they do progress to the top of their field, make sure they know who they are when they age out of their particular realm of fame and stardom.

We bumped into a family recently that we hadn't seen in years. Before a minute passed, we were launched into a verbal resume of all that their kids had and were accomplishing. Sports, academics, and music were covered in such a flurry of glowing pride that I couldn't help but feel I was standing in the presence of greatness. When the accolades were finished, the inevitable moment arrived and they turned to us and said, "So, what do your kids do?" Crap. I am not quick on my feet in moments like that. I stood stunned, with my mouth gaping open, until my husband stepped in and without missing a beat said, "Well, our oldest really likes horses and our youngest is an amazing snuggler. She is really getting good at it." You have never seen a conversation end so quickly. Excuses were made and we parted ways. This is just an example of how parents are interacting with each other these days. Instead of supporting each other and being honest with the ups and downs that come with parenting, everyone seems focused on appearing like they have nailed it and achieved success on every level.

Our girls repeated the first level of swimming lessons three times. Three times in Sea Stars because they both refused to put their heads underwater. Seriously. So, when they finally passed* it goes without saying that we needed

* Full disclosure—we bribed them with Dairy Queen.

a break from the public pool for a while. They eventually enrolled in Jelly Fish, but it was a few years later. Not going to lie, they were a lot bigger than the other kids in the class but oh well. I could have forced the lessons, done it quicker, been sterner, but you know what? It doesn't actually matter anymore. They eventually learned to swim, and they absolutely love it now. Maybe another family would have handled it differently and had that work out well for them. But this worked for our kids. And that is the point—all kids are different, so let's not throw them on a spectrum to compare and contrast all their skills and achievements. They have the rest of their lives for that. They don't need it from their parents.

You have to know what works for your family and for your kids and be confident in it. Your child will not have the same skills and gifts as another child and that is what makes children so wonderful and interesting and diverse. Your child may be a savant and excel at something in an extraordinary way. Nurture that. Support them in every way you can so they can be the best they can be. But don't make their value as a human being be that skill. Your child may not seem to have any particular gifts right now, but as they get older and mature, you will see talents and skills form in them. Nurture that too. Every child has their own timeline for development, and it does absolutely no favours to anyone for us to compare them and make them feel inadequate. This will not spur them into excellence, it will only damage them.

I will never forget when our youngest daughter started grade two. She was so eager to have it be her turn for all the wonderful things her big sister was getting to do and learn at school. She had the same teacher our older daughter had, so we set out to begin a new year feeling like we had a good idea of what to expect. One thing I have been learning, and it may be super obvious but I am going to say it anyway, is that what works for one of your children may not work for the other(s). I have to remind myself of this particularly frequently because our girls are very close in age, daily getting asked if they are twins, and they also get along uncannily well. But all of these similarities mask two very different personalities, especially when it comes to school. Our oldest is a daydreamer, is constantly being told to focus, and has had to really work at learning to apply herself. Our youngest is a perfectionist and will sit with her hand in the air until she is called on, where her sister will shout out because she is so excited to share. These are traits that I had to learn once they were in school. I am not overly hard on the girls about their school work. I don't put our daughter's "perfectionism" on her, because it is definitely an intrinsic trait. I couldn't control this any more than I could my oldest daughter's energetic nature. But I have to respect this trait and be aware of it so I don't set her up to be stressed and overwhelmed about school when she is older. She needs to be told to relax whereas her sister needs to be told to try harder. If I treated both girls the same with their school work, it would be disastrous.

Back to the start of grade two. We had been in school for about two weeks and piano lessons were starting back up as well. Our youngest daughter is extremely easygoing by nature, despite her perfectionism. She is consistent and reliable and content. So you can imagine my surprise when we were called into our first piano lesson of the term and my sweet girl threw her books on the ground and burst into tears exclaiming, "I can't learn to spell and do math and learn piano too!"

I was beyond shocked. I quietly apologized to the piano teacher, picked up the books, took my daughter by the hand and went outside for a walk. She shared with me that the teacher had been giving them a series of pretests that week to gauge where the students were so she could group them accordingly. My daughter thought that she was supposed to know everything on the assessment tests already and was, therefore, basically failing at grade two a couple of weeks into school, as the pages kept being returned full of mistakes. This same assessment would have been given to my oldest daughter, but it wasn't mentioned and definitely did not bother her. We withdrew from piano that week, along with our other activities and didn't resume them until after Christmas when grade two wasn't so overwhelming.

So, listen to your children. Forget about what level of karate Johnny is in and how good at violin little Suzy is. They aren't your kids. Your kids could never be average because they are your kids. Their excellence has nothing to do with their achievements. They might be really amazing at something, or they might not be. Either way—they are perfectly imperfect just the way they are.

PARENTING
PHILOSOFAIL

♡

PARENTING PHILOSOFAIL

·····································

PARENTING PHILOSOPHY + FAILURE

I have never read a parenting book. I own a couple, borrowed a few, got the odd one out from the public library,* but I have never actually read one. The two that I actually purchased were:

1. *Baby Sleep Solution* by Suzy Giodarno [9]
2. *Have a New Kid by Friday* by Dr. Kevin Leman[10]

The first book listed is often purchased by new mothers, and I am sure it is awesome and wise but the author made a critical mistake when choosing to write a book for brand-new moms as her target audience. I guess it depends if the author only cared that the book was purchased or if they actually wanted it to be read, because here is the thing … no new mother can stay awake to read. Not possible. The simple act of being horizontal makes most new moms fall asleep instantly. I am lucky to have even remembered the title of this book.

* Don't worry, Dad—I returned them. I think…

Sorry, Suzy—I never made it past the first page. It wasn't personal. It was survival. I am sure the book is wonderful! And for the record, I still did recommend it to many friends because the description on the back was excellent. Very inspiring. My confession also gives any new moms out there that are reading my book a free pass to doze off without hurting my feelings. I get it. Put the book down and go have a nap.

The second book I mentioned is focused more on older children and correcting unwanted behaviour. In all honesty, I did start the first chapter, and for no other reason than life getting in the way, I never got through it. My daughter saw this book sitting on our coffee table one day and after examining the title for a few minutes she turned to me, her eyes full of excitement and exclaimed, "Mommy! Are you having another baby?!" No. That is not what "Have a new kid by Friday" is about. And don't we wish it was that easy? Read this book and then *ta-da!* You have will have another child! Congratulations!

So those are my experiences with parenting books. If you are second-guessing your decision to buy my book, I will politely refer you back to the Introclaimer. I never set out intending this to be a "parenting book," and though you may disagree with me, I still don't really think it is. Yes, I relate a lot of these topics to children, but I continually point out that none of this will work if we do not have the same standards for ourselves. So in that regard, this is not a parenting book. Children and parenting are merely the examples used to address issues and shortcomings in our overall society. Our entire culture has become one that is lacking in the areas that I talk about in this book. Kindness, patience, confidence, responsibility, passion—we have become an apathetic nation that are glued to our phones and only care about ourselves. Harsh but true. Any stories you hear about acts of kindness seem to be viewed as exceptional actions, instead of being the expectation of behavior and human interaction. So when I talk about instilling your kids with the values that will make them kindfident, you have to intentionally work on yourself as well. You will have to have a teachable spirit and be able to honestly look inward to see where you need to improve. We all have something that we can be better at, and your kids will notice you making an effort as you begin to ask new things of them.

The reason I do not want to refer to these ideals as a parenting philosophy is because I believe these are no more than basic human traits that we have gotten away from. A philosophy is the study of a particular system of philosophical thought. Whereas I believe these basic principles could be adopted into anyone's life, regardless of their religion, ethnicity, socioeconomic status, or otherwise. This is how things should be and the fact that we, as a culture, have moved away from these principles does not dismiss the fact that they are the backbone of a healthy society.

I have no specific parenting philosophy of my own, but I have heard many mentioned over the years, so it seems like you have a lot to choose from if you aren't really connecting with this book. Here are a few for you to consider:

- Attachment Parenting [11]
- Authoritarian Parenting [12]
- Holistic Parenting [13]
- Permissive Parenting [14]
- Positive Parenting [15]

- Helicopter Parenting [16]
- Free-Range Parenting [17]
- Dolphin Parenting [18]

If I absolutely had to pick one of these, I would pick Dolphin Parenting. It sounds quite lovely:

"The Dolphin Parent: Dolphin parents are the balance of extremes. They're collaborative and have rules and expectations, but they also encourage independence and creativity. Like the dolphin, they're firm and flexible and use their community to nurture their child's nature."

- www.parenting.com/parenting-advice

Not bad, right? So again, no hard feelings if you want to jump ship from Kindfident Parenting to Dolphin Parenting. And how cute are dolphins* by the way?

Okay, so it sounds like maybe I have just created a new philosophy after all. Dolphkident Parenting. Yes,nailed it! I think this is definitely going to catch on.

All joking aside, the main point I am trying to make here is that these are not new, groundbreaking concepts that I am presenting. These are fundamental traits that we all need to find our way back to in order to rebuild our narcissistic culture that is on the verge of spiraling out of control. We need to go back to the basics. All of us—kids *and* adults. We need to reinstate a higher standard of expectations for our

* We named our first daughter after a dolphin, but that's another story.

behaviour that will spark a positive change in our culture. We have drifted so far from a society that cares for one another in authentic and consistent ways. If buying a coffee for the person in the car behind you is the ultimate standard for kindness, then we have a long way to go. Don't get me wrong, I love "pay it forward" gestures and have done this myself, but we need to dig much deeper than this if we are really going to make a difference in our families, schools, communities, and society as a whole.

So let's stop worrying so much about which parenting philosophy we want to practice on our children and start thinking more about what kind of people we all need to be without putting all the expectations for the future on our kids' shoulders. It's about time we all took the responsibility and began to share it among ourselves as a whole.

They say when you have a child that it "takes a village'." I love this saying and try to embody it in my home—North America seems like the only culture that doesn't embrace intergenerational family structures. It seems like the North American ideal is to turn of age and go out on your own into the world, leaving all trace of your family unit behind you. This doesn't seem like success to me—it seems isolated and lonely and selfish. Don't get me wrong, I believe strongly in children growing up and maturing and finding their own lives and independence, but the notion of isolated independence being the measure of success seems sad and empty to me. I believe it also speaks to the brokenness of the family unit in our culture. Other cultures honour their elders and nurture their parental and sibling relationships long past the moment they are legally allowed to live on their own. They respect their aunts, uncles, and grandparents, take care of one another as they age, are widowed, become sick or none of the above—but regardless, family is valued.

Honouring and embracing family does not equal dependence, immaturity, or stagnant development. These are often lumped together in our culture—in order to become a successful adult, you have to move on from your family. It is impossible for me to believe that the proper timeline for parenting is zero to eighteen.

I graduated at seventeen and like most wide-eyed graduates, I was overjoyed and excited at the options that were laid out before me. I decided to go away for a one-year program at a Bible College before settling into my degree at University. My parents had my brother and me when they were quite young, and so when they drove off after settling me into my new college (where my brother was also attending), they were officially empty nesters at the ripe old age of for-ty-one. Sheesh—I have friends who have had babies at forty-one. The thing is, parents are parents no matter how young they are, and it honestly did not cross my mind that they may have been devastated at the stage they had suddenly entered at such a young age.

Teenagers are generally selfish by nature, and so I don't feel overly guilty about not recognizing their sadness at the time—but I feel it is worth mentioning, because the fact that they did not put guilt on me is actually the reason I am sharing this story. You see, my mom was heartbroken when she drove away from my brother and me that day. She only told me a few years ago that she cried the entire ten-hour drive home. But, in the same way that I never mentioned my daughter's forgotten hug, she never men-tioned her sorrow that day, because it would have cast a shadow on a healthy milestone of independence in my life. I, like my children, am very sensitive, and I am pretty sure that if my mom made me aware of how she was feeling leading up to my departure, I may have second guessed going away to school, and the experience would have become one of stress instead of joy.

She would have never wanted to hold me back, and so she just cried herself home. She never mentioned to me how sad she was, she just counted the days until we came home for Thanksgiving. This is the way we are supposed to love our children. Love them so they become strong and kind and independent and confident and then let them go into the world without guilt or manipulation. Set them free, and then have a place for them in your home and your heart for the rest of their lives. Obviously I don't have a room of my own at my parents' house now—that would be weird—but until I was married I knew I had a place there, no matter what. With this place came the freedom to be an adult and the security of being a daughter. Though I never lived at home full time after graduating, I never felt like I didn't have a place in my family. My parents were the absolute epitome of support as I chased my dreams. I was allowed independence from them as I grew older, but continued to have a healthy, growing relationship with them as our roles all changed over the years.

There is an island off the coast of Greece called Ikaria[19] that is known for having the longest life expectancy in the world. There have been many studies about what makes this island a place where people live well into their hundreds with not only healthy bodies but minds as well. There are many factors that have been credited, including the Mediterranean diet, naps, wine and weather—but two things that stood out to me were family and farming. Ikarian people live, like many people in Europe, in the same communities (not the same houses—let's not get carried away…) as their immediate family and extended relatives. This intergenerational living creates a deep sense of community that we are designed to be part of. It supports you and gives you a place that you are accepted and loved, so that you can be fulfilled internally and not just superficially. The second point that I found interesting was related to farming. When you live and work on your own land, planting crops and growing your own food, it is not only healthy and active but literally prepares people for the next season of life.

About ten years ago my parents decided to follow through on a dream they have had for a long time, to start an olive grove and eventually press the very first olive oil in Canada. It has caused quite the buzz of interest, along with equal doses of excitement and skepticism. They were interviewed about their farm recently for a magazine and my dad said, "You plant a vineyard for your children and an olive grove for your grandchildren." This comment perfectly combines the two points of intentional living that caught my interest about Ikaria, and combines them in a way that reminds us that life isn't all about "you" but the legacy of those who will come in the generations after you. Obviously we can't all farm our own land and grow our own food, but the point is to be intentional with the way we live. You have to live with intention, with passion, and in a vibrant community filled with love. Don't just get through each day—live each day presently, intentionally, and look forward to tomorrow.

My family knows that I love using the term "YOLO"* as often as possible. You Only Live Once. Nerdy but awesome.

So, let's take a step away from all of these specific philosophies and look back into our past, to the way we were created to live so we can have the most vibrant and joyful life possible. Separating our "parenting styles" with these individual labels divides us instead of focuses us on the fact that we are all in this together and should have a common goal for a greater good. The point is that there are a million different ways to do things. But there is no one perfect way to do them. And thank goodness for that! We need to remember what really matters and not get caught up in labels and perfection. Love your family. Love your kids. Mean what you say. Do the best you can. The rest will fall into place.

* There may or may not have been a situation on a family holiday recently where I yelled "YOLO" and ran off the hiking trail and straight into the ocean fully clothed.

UNIFORMANIA

♡

UNIFORMANIA

··

UNIFORM + MANIA

I love where our girls go to school. Not only does it have unbelievable teachers, genuine community spirit, and an amazing parent group—it also has a really lovely campus … sprawling grounds, stately brick buildings, a clock tower … and, of course, uniforms. Having two girls, I am a huge fan of uniforms. They only have three decisions to make each morning: red, white, or blue shirt. I cannot imagine having to get two girls ready for school each morning with a free range of closet choices. It would be a nightmare.* So, this is the uniform drill—plaid skirt, collared shirt, navy knee socks and black shoes. Classic, modest, lovely.

The whole concept of uniforms, other than to look adorable, is that they are supposed to be a social leveler. They are meant to take away the pressure to have the perfect clothes for school and at the same time minimize the social cliques that seem to form largely based on name brands and fashion.

* Nightmare in a "first-world problems" sort of way…

Unfortunately, as darling as uniforms are, kids are kids and if you take away their clothing as a form of self-expression and status, they will find another way. And in the realm of uniforms, the alternate route of self-expression is accessories. Backpacks, shoes, jackets, school supplies, water bottles ... there are a million name brands that still come into play, even with basic clothing options being taken out of the equation. Uniforms may help, but they don't magically solve the problem of appearance-based judgment and the pressure to be fashionable at school.

We need to address the real problem, not just the clothes. Human nature runs deep, and for some reason looks and appearance are often the basis for the formation of social cliques. So, yes, we can level the playing field with things like uniforms, but we need to teach our children long before this to counterbalance our human instinct to judge others superficially.

Children are not born knowing how to judge others. It is a learned behaviour and more often than not, it is learned from within our homes. So, again with the repetitive theme of this book, you first have to look at yourself before examining your child's behaviour. Of course, these are human beings we are talking about, not robots, so there is always the exception to the rule, but generally the apple does not fall far from the tree. If you are always fussing about clothes, unhappy with your appearance (or too happy with it—equally problematic!) and generally consumed with the way you look, chances are that your child is going to absorb these values in one way or another. This is not exclusive to girls. Boys can be just as vain* as girls, but it is generally more prevalent in the culture of girls.

* My daughters and I are always waiting for my husband. Always.

Humans have always been vain. There isn't a period of time throughout the history of the world that is without vanity. I would be willing to bet that even in the Garden of Eden, Adam and Eve fussed about which leaves they should cover themselves with after realizing they probably shouldn't be walking around naked. Curly edge or straight? Dark green or light green?* Yes, vanity runs deep. There is, of course, healthy and important aspects of vanity. It is often a large part of what drives us to stay in shape, eat well, and practice good hygiene. So, thank goodness for that. But it is also a huge part of what makes people feel insecure and worthless. Or arrogant and superior.

Like so many other things in life, if you base your self-worth on something meaningless like fashion, name brands, or what size jeans you wear, you are setting yourself up for inevitable failure and disappointment. Because there will always be a new style, a better name brand, and a smaller size of jeans.

In every home we have lived in, my mom always had the poem "Desiderata"[20] up somewhere in our house, quietly offering wisdom on a wide range of topics, all of which are just as, if not more, relevant today as when it was written almost one hundred years ago. One of my favourite lines of the poem is:

"IF YOU COMPARE YOURSELF WITH OTHERS,
YOU MAY BECOME VAIN OR BITTER, FOR ALWAYS
THERE WILL BE GREATER AND LESSER PERSONS
THAN YOURSELF."

-"Desiderata"

* I have no evidence to back this theory up.

Now, more than ever, we need a reminder of this wisdom. Within our materialistic world of social media, magazines, fashion, cars, and houses comes an unspoken need to compare ourselves to others. Nothing makes someone become dissatisfied quicker than comparing themselves with someone else. Or overconfident, depending on who or what you are comparing yourself to. "YOU WILL BECOME EITHER VAIN OR BITTER," the poem warns. Vain or bitter. Yuck. Neither of those are words that I am personally striving to be or want for my children. I am willing to bet that you agree with me.

Yet we continue to build lives that center on materialistic things. The importance placed upon name brands seems to have reached a whole new level. I think that with the culture of uniforms in our school, I notice it even more. And in complete honesty, I am a bit of a sucker for name brands myself. The thing is, not unlike social media, it doesn't do any good to tell our kids that fashion and name brands and all the other things they are navigating in school, don't matter. Sure, we can tell our kids that, but it is not going to resonate with them. What it will do is confirm in their minds that you do not understand them and that you have, in fact, completely forgotten what it was like to be a kid. Don't tell them it doesn't matter. Tell them that you remember feeling the same way, wanting the coolest things, feeling like you want to fit in and to feel good about the way you look. That is the first step in not putting yourself out to pasture as an irrelevant source of wisdom. The second step is to remind them that all the stuff they so desperately want doesn't define them and won't make them happy. That it doesn't make them better than other people. That it is just stuff. This is what we need to be teaching our kids.

In the same way that we can't hide our kids from social media, we have to teach our kids how to successfully deal with the pressure that fashion, name brands, and materialism is going to play in their lives. And in order to help them understand it, we have to acknowledge that it exists.

That is the most important step in beginning to diffuse the power that it could potentially hold over them.

The next step is to tell them that no matter how much they want something, they can't have everything they desire. This needs to be modeled as well, of course, not an easy thing to do in our society of instant gratification and enormous debt-to-income ratios. Another important aspect that needs to be mentioned is that this doesn't have anything to do with your household income. Just because you can, doesn't mean you should. Say no to your kids, even if you can afford to buy them the best of everything the world has to offer. And if you can't afford all the things your kids are begging for, tell them that. Be transparent with them. Don't go into debt trying to satisfy your children's desire for the newest item they can't live without. Because next month there is going to be a new item, a better name brand, a shinier object. If your kids begin to define themselves with these items instead of the things that really matter, they will have a hard time finding that true inner confidence that we have been talking about. They will be learning to base their self-worth on a false confidence and will be creating a foundation that changes and shifts with each fleeting trend that our culture entices us with.

Once you have established* yourself as a relevant being in your child's life, you can then go on to be the quiet voice

* Or re-established.

in their head that gently reminds them that these "things" aren't what gives them value. They don't make them better or worse than anyone else. Yes, this "stuff" will always be there, knocking on the door of their self-worth, but it is up to us to fill up our children with confidence in themselves inwardly not outwardly. Only then can they begin to understand and grasp the balance of having fun with self-expression and style without letting it own or define them.

Now, I have to be honest here, and tell you that my own kids can quite often be seen wearing names brands. I would hate it if anyone reading this knows me and is thinking, "hypocrite." Our closets are full of name brands—truth. Honestly, I am a bit of a sucker for name brands, for myself but especially for my kids. It is always so much cuter in a smaller size! So yes, they have the cool backpacks and the right shoes. But they also have a whole bunch of hand-me-downs. And stuff from Walmart. And name brands. It is all a balance. And so long as they are happy to wear all of these items, then I don't mind at all buying them the cool name brands too. They just need to learn the difference of knowing who they are on the inside versus fabricating an outside image of who they want to be. Teach your kids that their value comes from internal principles not from external items.

It probably goes without saying, but of course they need to know they will be loved and accepted regardless of what they decide their personal style choices are. Hopefully those choices don't include piercings and tattoos but if they do, you are going have to love them through it.

When I was younger, the trend with female Hollywood celebrities was the pixie cut. It was fresh and fun and looked super cute on screen, paired with the perfect clothes and makeup that comes with being a movie star. So of course, my nineteen-year-old self decided this was a great look and was the perfect choice for me to switch things up from my signature waist-long hair that I'd had my entire life until that point. So, off I went, with my magazine clippings of Gwyneth Paltrow and Winona Ryder and a dozen other beautiful movie starts and their perfect pixie cuts. An hour later, I left the hair salon in tears, with what slightly resembled a brush cut that had been blown dry and half-heartedly pat down with some putty. My new short hair stubbornly refused to lay down against my scalp and instead chose to point straight up towards the heavens, in a seemingly defiant gesture, to greet the world with my new look. Not only did I look nothing like the women on the magazine pages that were now crumpled in the garbage, I looked nothing like myself. After a few days of wallowing in self-pity and hiding in my room, I decided to try to work with what I had and make the best of it. Perhaps a nose piercing would go with my new short 'do. Maybe heavier eye liner and darker lipstick would ensure that people still knew I was a girl. So there I was, cropped hair, pierced nose, and heavily made up. Of course I had the privilege of having a front row seat to this experiment of self-expression, but when I saw my then ten-year-old cousin for the first time since sporting my new look, she literally froze in shock. There she stood—open mouth, big blue eyes round and unblinking—and finally after a few very awkward moments, she looked at my mom and spluttered, "Oh, Auntie, you must be so disappointed!" Ouch. But my sweet mom simply slipped her arm around my waist and replied, "When you have a daughter this lovely, it doesn't matter what she looks like." Thanks, Mom. I am fairly positive that she didn't love my new look, not that I did either, but I knew without a doubt she loved me. Unconditionally.

And so the years continued to pass by, my hair (slowly) grew out, I decided the nose ring needed to go and I learned how to do my makeup with a slightly less gothic flair—and somewhere along the way I eventfully found my own personal style. I made more than a few mistakes along the way, but I learned that my self-worth is a very separate entity than my self- expression. Thank goodness.

So, let your kids have fun with their style and their clothes. Find a balance with name brands. There is nothing wrong with wanting to look "cool" as long as it doesn't define you. And please, don't buy your kids everything they ask for, and definitely don't ever let them think that what they wear makes them who they are, for better or for worse.

RELIGAPOINTMENT

....

♡

RELIGAPOINTMENT

....

RELIGION + DISAPPOINTMENT

My kids hate the Christian radio station. I feel so bad seeing this in writing let alone knowing that other people* are going to see it. I am aware that this comment opens me up to judgment, but this book is, among other things, about being transparent. So, now you know—my kids hate the Christian radio station. I struggled with this for a while. When I would drive with other families, and their kids were happily bopping away to the heart-warming tunes on the radio, I felt I had failed in some way as I thought of the protests that my girls emit when I turn the same station on in our car. The thing is, my girls love music. Really love it. Music is a huge part of our life—every road trip or special event has a soundtrack to accompany it. We all love finding just the right song to suit the mood of a particular activity. Playlists are an integral part of our life, whether they are for Saturday morning pancakes or our family's Ugly Sweater Christmas party. So when I realized that there was

* I know for sure that at least my parents will read this. And my husband. They kinda have to.

dissension among the ranks when it came to Christian music, I was surprised and, to be honest, a little disappointed.

There have been a few clues along the way, so I am assuming it is no surprise that our family is Christian, but it is very important to me that this is not a "religious book." I actually don't think this book has anything to do with being a Christian and everything to do with being a human. Being a Christian does not actually make you kind. I never went to church as a child, and wasn't raised in a Christian home. Our family started going to church when I was in high school, and at that point I realized that we had been raised with the standards and morals of Christianity without realizing it. There are really good people who don't believe in God, just as there are really crummy people who say they are Christians. And then there are super awesome people who are also Christians. So if I was to launch this book under the genre of Christian writing, I strongly believe that there would be some people that would not read it based simply on the fact that it was in the "religious" section. Because they may have experienced Religapointment before and now won't even bother looking in the religious section of the bookstore. And then they would miss out on the phenomenal experience that you are currently having, reading this wise and insightful book.

So yes, I am a Christian. But guess what? I was a 'good' person before I was a Christian too. The difference is that now I feel like I know where my desire to be kind and good comes from. For me, it comes from my faith. This may not be true for every person, and I have repeatedly said that the traits I talk about need to be the backbone of our society, regardless of your religion, ethnicity, culture, and beliefs. So yes, these traits can all be inextricably tied to Christianity, but they can also be separated from it.

I am obviously not a religious scholar but in my opinion* it is an uncompromising fact that people can be good outside of religion, and so I back my previous statement. This is not a religious book. The problem with religion is that you will almost inevitably, at some point, be disappointed in some aspect of it. The thing that is commonly misunderstood, though, is that the disappointment isn't with the religion, it is with the people. People are the vessels that religion is translated through, and we are flawed so, therefore, religion is inevitably flawed. You aren't supposed to measure the value of Christianity by its people, because people will always make mistakes. This is actually kind of freeing— and the point of my faith. We aren't supposed to be perfect and do it all on our own. Thank goodness. I now know where my joy comes from, but if you are not a Christian, every single thing I talk about in this book still applies to you, because I am pretty sure you are human. So, there you go—you can't argue with that.

Back to my kids hating the Christian radio station. I had decided, unbeknown to them, that our drives to school and activities should be to the soundtrack of our local Christian station. I have driven for many school field trips and more than once had a child say that they were only allowed to listen to the Christian station. I tried to make it a subtle shift, having it playing quietly before they got in the car, but within minutes, the

* I have been watching a lot of legal shows lately and they always seem to end with "in my opinion" so they don't get criticized for being overly opinionated and underinformed. Clever, right?

complaining started. I did not want to recreate the song drama that I talked about in Niceschlappen, because that would make listening to Christian music a punishment. I really didn't want it to be a battle, and so I changed it. The next day, I had it playing again and the response was the same. This time I asked the question, "Why don't you guys like this music?" The answer surprised me. My oldest daughter said simply, "Because Jesus is supposed to make you feel joyful and this music has no joy* in it." Hmmmm. I couldn't argue with that. The music actually was a bit dreary. I realized in that moment that it wasn't the Christian music they hated, it was the style of Christian music. Wow, am I glad I stopped to ask the question. It saved me from a battle I did not want to fight and did not need to. So we have since found some wonderful, peppy Christian music that the girls love and sing their hearts out to. But we also listen to country music, Jack Johnson, the *Guardians of the Galaxy* soundtracks, and when my husband is in the car, Flo Rida. Seriously. There are so many types of great music, and it is not wrong to enjoy them. Music is powerful, so choose good stuff but don't worry about only listening to the Christian station because that is legalistic and unnecessary. In my opinion.

I made a mistake by thinking that listening only to the Christian station would make my children better kids. That was wrong. Kids can listen to the "right" music all day long and if the parental guidance in their home isn't kind and

* Remember this is the raw opinion of a child. Obviously there are some lovely and joyful songs on the Christian Station—we just seemed to turn it on every time there was something playing that was a wee bit more like a traditional hymn or old school quartet.

authentic and consistent, that music isn't going to help them. So don't get caught up in the details. We all make mistakes. Christians, atheists, agnostics—we all make mistakes. What matters is what we do after. How we try to right the wrongs we have done. How we learn from these mistakes. Don't measure religion by the people that follow it. That is a recipe for disappointment. Because we are allowed to fail. Every day. Mistakes are a guarantee. So find comfort in that instead of disappointment. It would be a lot bleaker of a situation if we were all expected to be perfect.

PART TWO

BELLY BREATHING

♡

BELLY BREATHING

....

Babies are born knowing how to belly breathe. At some point, we forget how to belly breathe and begin breathing shallow little breaths into our chest, hunching our shoulders, jutting out our chins, and all the other bad habits that we will have to learn how to correct one day. If you watch sleeping infants, their little tummies will rise and fall in perfect rhythm. It is almost hypnotizing how exact it is. The point is that we are born knowing how to do it flawlessly. Belly breathing is the single most effective way to get oxygen into our bloodstream, and oxygen is the fastest way for all of our body's cells to make adenosine triphosphate (ATP), which is the real energy currency of the body. It is amazing that this is a skill we are born with ... and it is a skill that we lose as we get older.

I went for a massage* the other day, and the masseuse was explaining to me the importance of remembering how to belly breathe. Remembering how to do something is very different than learning a new skill. It is in our muscle

* This does not happen very often, just FYI.

memory already, we just have to be intentional about recon-
necting with this memory before we can experience the
peace and benefit that this skill can bring to our bodies.
You need to be aware of the different parts of your body
and how they are designed to work together in harmony
to bring ultimate benefit to your overall being. Tension
breeds tension, and release breeds release, giving either
systematic decline or improvement to your whole body. In
the same way, we need to be aware of being intentional with
all the parts of our families and bring awareness to the roles
each member plays. When we acknowledge each person in
our family unit as an invaluable part of the group, family
identity blossoms and peace and unity start to permeate
in the same way that breathing the way you were designed
to brings the perfect balance of oxygen to your body.

When you really concentrate on the way you breathe,
you start to notice things you hadn't before. Like maybe
forgetting to breathe altogether. Especially when you
are frustrated and tired. Instead of inhaling deeply
and being intentional about your patience, you hold
your breath and react without thought. This approach
can be some of the most harmful parenting that we
do—reactive parenting, without thought or intention.
But if you can learn to take a breath in that split second
before you enter the zone where anger will control your
parenting, you will be amazed at what a huge difference
that one simple change can make in your family.

There is nothing wrong with being stern with your kids.
I could probably* be a little more stern with my kids, but
the key thing about discipline is to never discipline in anger.

* Definitely.

That is when damage is done and wounds are created. Your kids need to know what the rules are if they are expected to play the game well. Disciplining in anger means that you have forgotten to be intentional. Make solid rules in your home with corresponding, solid consequences. Make the punishment fit the crime. Be open with your kids so they know what the punishment will be for their mistakes. Of course, your kids will make mistakes you don't expect, just like we did to our parents. We can't predict the future and kids aren't robots. You can't punch in an equation that guarantees perfect behaviour from them. Instead, in the most realistic way possible, communicate your expectations to your children and let them know what will happen when they fall short of those expectations—and then follow through with what you have said. And, of course—the common thread for the success of all of this—expect it of yourself as well.

The old saying "Do what I say, not as I do" is a recipe for creating a rebellious child that doesn't respect authority. Respect cannot be demanded, it has to be earned. From small things like making your bed, to bigger things like iPhone and internet use, to really big things like honesty and integrity. This will not work if the whole family does not have the same standard of expectation and commitment as a whole to keep each other accountable.

Our bodies are also born knowing how to react to pain. It is defense system that is hardwired into us. If we did not react involuntarily to pain, then we would not be able to react in a way to protect ourselves. Interestingly enough, the brain itself has no pain receptors. It is a series of pain receptors on the bones and scalp that signal pain. The body is designed to give compounding clues and signals to you that something is wrong, before you actually register physical pain. If you ignore the series   of signals and warnings that you are being given, you can end up dealing with a greater amount of pain than if you were able to respond at the first signal. When you become acutely aware of listening to your body and responding appropriately to minimize the chance of discomfort, you will discover a systemic improvement in your overall well-being and health.

Our families also give us signals to the overall health of how we are functioning as a unit. Like the body, there are a series of compounding clues that something is wrong before there is a visible breakdown that has to be addressed. If we can work at being aware of the small indicators we are receiving from our children, then we have a greater chance at diffusing a bigger, more painful situation before it arises. Children do not go from carefree to troubled overnight. They will give you signals that something is wrong, possibly even before they know what it is. It is our responsibility to pay attention to these clues before they overwhelm our children and they no longer know how to explain what has gone wrong.

When our daughter gurgled her first word, we were thrilled and amazed at the slobbery miracle we had just witnessed. My sweet mother said something to me that day that I found impossible to comprehend. She said, "There are going to be moments you are going to wish she never started talking." Sure enough, Mom was right*. There are days that I literally cannot get a word in between my two beautiful girls' steady stream of chatter. And honestly, it isn't always what you want to spend hours listening too. But

---

*Sorry girls—no offense meant.

in those moments that I am listening attentively, actively engaged in every tedious details of the newest Calico Family that just came out, I remind myself of one simple, grounding truth:

> If you don't listen to the small stuff, why would they tell you the big stuff?

This simple statement gives me peace on days where I struggle with wanting a few minutes to myself but am caught up in endless detailed conversations on topics that don't overly captivate me. Because to them—in that moment, at that age—they are topics of extreme importance and them choosing to share the details with me is confirmation that I am still their most trusted confidant. The stories may not seem important, but they are. So listen to your children. Sit down with them and really listen about their day, who played with whom and what their friends had in their lunches. If you can establish an environment of healthy sharing in your home when your kids are younger, they will continue to share with you as they get older and the topics get more complicated. But if you don't put the time in and listen to the small stuff, don't be surprised when you aren't the person they come to with the big stuff.

Spend time with your family—real time, not just sitting in front of the TV or rushing around to the next activity. This is when you will learn to be aware of the different signals each member of your family gives you to indicate if they are a happy and healthy part of your family unit. Be aware of subtle changes so you can diffuse problems as they arise. And through all of it, don't forget to breathe.

TURBULENCE

♡

TURBULENCE

....

I hate flying. I don't remember hating it as a kid, but somewhere along the road from childhood to adulthood I suddenly became painfully aware of how incredibly vulnerable you are bouncing around at thirty thousand feet. I am well aware of all the statistical evidence proving air travel to be safer than driving a car, but it doesn't make me feel any better. Here's the thing though—I love vacations. I know that's a pretty common statement, but I love them in a borderline unhealthy way. I am a total vacation-a-holic. As soon as we are back from one holiday, I am obsessed with planning the next one. It doesn't have to be anytime soon, but just knowing that sometime in the next couple of years I will get to experience the unparalleled bliss of a family vacation helps me sleep better at night.* Here's the thing though ... you can't have the beach vacation without the airplane (not where we live, anyway). You have to do the stuff you don't want to do in order to enjoy the good stuff.

* Not that I need help—see * on page 34.

Even though I hate to fly, I would never consider not booking a trip, because I know the destination will be worth it. In the same way, you are never going to experience the full joy of parenthood unless you are willing to do the hard work. Nobody* likes to discipline their kids. It is easier to ignore bad behaviour than to address it, especially when it is close to bedtime, if you are on the way out the door, at a restaurant … the list goes on. But if you start to pick and choose when to follow through on consequences, to turn a blind eye, to give second chances until your children are suddenly calling the shots, it will start to create a pattern of behaviour that is hard to correct. Intermittent reinforcement is the quickest way to create a stubborn child. If you say "no" three times and then "yes" on the fourth time, as your child begs for whatever the desired item of the moment is, you have committed the crime of N.I.R.** You have just taught your child that you will give in after three tries. The next time your precious child sets their sights on something and you say "no" they will think that after three tries, they will hear a "yes." So if and when you don't give in after three times, there is inevitably going to be a battle of wills. Turbulence. A bumpy moment between parent and child. Fasten your seat belt and take a breath. Are you going to avoid the bumps or hang in there until things smooth out?

The thing about turbulence is there is no way of knowing how long it will last. It may be a few small bumps, or it could get very bad and last a long time.

* At least I am assuming nobody that is reading this book likes to discipline their kids. Yikes, there are other genres for that.

** Negative Intermittent Reinforcement.

Either way, you have to wait it out. Don't give into your child's demands. If you say "no" once and they ask twenty more times, then you have to commit to saying it twenty-one times. And then be willing to wait out the bumps. The more consistent you are, the less they will ask you over and over because at some point your "no" is taken seriously. They know that no means no.*

N.I.R is particularly dangerous to the success of your parenting because it has the ability to undermine an enormous amount of good. You may have been extremely patient and consistent for weeks, embracing the bumps along the way as you stayed true to your no's and your consequences and then BAM—the end of the week rolls around and in a moment of exhaustion you give in (because you are human). In that moment of weakness, you have set back all the consistency that you have been building.

The good news is that this process is normal, and we all have those moments of weakness. Maybe you just want an easy bed time for once, so you let them talk you into one more story (or four more...been there, done that) or maybe you are out for dinner, so you give in and order dessert to avoid them making a scene in public. Either way, if you have said no once and then gave in you have committed N.I.R. and the power balance has shifted in favour of your child. Fortunately, we are smarter than our children so if this is where you are at right now, it's okay—get a good night's sleep and tomorrow is another day.

* When my girls were smaller, I made up an awesome song called "No Means No." The best part is that the song still works because the mere threat of me bursting into this lyrical masterpiece is enough to make them stop begging for whatever it is they are currently asking for.

We've all done it, and preventing N.I.R. from becoming a pattern is half the battle. The other half is doing up your seat belt and hanging in there through the turbulence as your child begins the long journey of accepting your new resolve.

As you devote yourself to no longer committing N.I.R., you need to know that P.I.R.* also exists. Learning how to use this effectively will help you keep the upper hand and ensure the power balance stays where it should be. On your side. When you see your little angels doing things in a way that makes your heart soar—reward them. P.I.R. isn't a prize for doing what's expected of them—this would eventually create entitled children—it is to be used wisely in situations where nothing specific was asked of them and they went above and beyond.

P.I.R isn't meant to be a huge reward, so don't go rushing out to buy a pony for your princess because she put her dishes in the dishwasher without being asked. It may be as simple as letting them watch a bedtime show on a school night because they had an especially good attitude while doing their homework or some other simple task. The point is to acknowledge positive behaviour that you haven't specifically asked for.

P.I.R. is the main reason that I don't give my kids an allowance. Don't get me wrong—I have given my girls money to do extra chores or other tasks that need to be done but not on a regular basis. Once you start paying a child to make their bed or clean their room, you are setting an expectation that they don't need to be an active member of your family unit unless they are getting compensated for it.

* Positive Intermittent Reinforcement.

There are things that your kids should be expected to do for no reason other than because they are a part of the family. Go ahead and give them little extras here and there, but a weekly allowance for doing the bare minimum is going to backfire when you start asking more of them as they get older. If you have chosen to give your kids an allowance in your home, don't feel like you have made a huge mistake that can't be undone. You have two options*:

1. Keep the allowance but change the expectations. Ask enough of them to justify the payment by doing things that are not just daily household tasks (chances are they will soon be happy with you canceling all of the new tasks along with the allowance and you will then be able to start fresh).
2. Cancel the allowance and tell them you are going to pay them for extra chores at a rate you come up with together (e.g., five dollars for weeding the driveway, two dollars for cleaning the baseboards, etc.).

What you want to remember is that it isn't wrong to reward your child for work. You just don't want to give them money for doing the bare minimum. This lack of expectation will risk turning your child into one of those adults** that expects an award for showing up to work on time.

* Assuming that you agree with my thoughts on allowance. If you disagree, no problem. Feel free to skip this section – no hard feelings.

** Reminder: the goal of all this is to raise successful adults.

So there you have it. You have been warned about the dangers of N.I.R. and the powers of P.I.R. You may feel like I have diverted off topic, but it is important to remember that the atmosphere that we create in our homes is inextricably linked to the way our children behave, in the present and the future. The old adage of "you are a product of your environment" is the main point here. Make your home a place where you do what you say, no means no, and you are expected to participate as an active member of your family unit without monetary reimbursement. And once again, as I have mentioned before—these values are not exclusively for your children. They don't work unless you have the same standards for you and your spouse.

It is worth repeating that the bumps may (probably) get worse before they get better. But the more consistent you are, the shorter this "turbulence" will last as your child begins the long journey of learning that "no means no."* So buckle up and hang in there until the "fasten seat belt" sign turns off. And think of that beautiful paradise you are heading to.

* I am dying to belt out the "No" song... It's really catchy. Maybe if this ever becomes an audio book, I'll include it as a feature.

SMALL TOWNS
+
COUNTRY MUSIC

♡

SMALL TOWNS + COUNTRY MUSIC

....

"On the eighth day God made country girls."
          -*Dean Brody* [21]

I grew up in a small town. My parents intentionally relocated our family to the country in search of a slower pace of life. We literally could not see another house from ours, unless it was dark and then you might see a faint glimmer of a faraway home nestled in its own space, far from traffic lights, corner stores, and the hustle and bustle of city life. We never closed our blinds because needing privacy from the neighbours was a concept that we did not have to worry about. The view from our deck would take your breath away. Every day brought some new magic to the foothills and mountains that sprawled out in front of our home. It was very idyllic and a huge part of who I am today is because I grew up in the country. Now this is either going to sound appealing to you or utterly horrendous. I get that we are all wired differently and that is okay. If you are one of those mysterious people that love the city—it's alright. You are still allowed to read this chapter, and I hope that you will still find some value in it, regardless of whether you are a city or a country person. The thing to realize is that I am using the "country" as a metaphor for social interaction. You don't need to live in the country, or even want to live in the country to act like "small town folk," which is what I am going to challenge you and your kids to try.

The reason that country living and small towns are so romanticized is because they come with a sense of nostalgia about a time that was simpler. People knew their neighbours, they helped each other without being asked and without resentment, or the expectation of anything in return. Store owners knew the names of the kids that frequented their shops.* You waved at each other, made eye contact, let your kids play in the street while the family dog romped around, unleashed. Listen to almost any country song and you will hear references to this type of living.**

The thing is I don't live in the country anymore. I always assumed that I would raise my own family in the country and recreate the type of childhood that I had. But life doesn't always work out the way you plan*** and that is totally okay. Sometimes it works out better and sometimes

* I was in our local grocery store the other day and the lady at the till asked me to tell my dad that his favorite cookies were back in stock. How sweet is that?

** And a whole lot of drinking, cheating, and heartache but I am going to ignore that because it totally doesn't fit into the theme of this chapter.

*** Sorry—spoiler alert.

it doesn't, but the balance is found in trying not to have overly detailed expectations for the future. Goals are fine, but unrealistic expectations will most likely result in disappointment. So yes, I assumed I would live in the country, but instead I live in an adorable small town across from a farm, and that is lovely for now. Maybe one day we will have land and more space, maybe we won't—either is fine because what I have learned is I can still raise my girls with these simple, old-fashioned values regardless of where we live. Country, city, or in between. It is not where you live, it's how you live.

I definitely err on the side of idealistic, but I am not so naive to forget that we have to teach our children "stranger danger" and all the other things that come along with imparting healthy boundaries and general safety guidelines. What I am suggesting is to simply remember that we are all human, and we are all trying to do our best at whatever stage of life we are in.

So say hi to your neighbours. Stop and buy lemonade from the kids down the street. Don't ask for change. Pet your neighbour's dog. If you don't like the way it smells, wash your hands after. These are not bizarre, scary concepts that are impossible to implement, they are simply going back to the basics. These are not just for those living in small towns; they are for those living in communities— which we all are, in one way or another. A man at school this morning, who didn't speak a word of English, held up his umbrella over me and walked me to my car. Made my day. Such a simple, lovely example of community.

If you don't model kindness, then how can you possibly ask it of your children? If you treat others badly, or not even badly but are indifferent to them, how do you think your kids are going to treat the other kids at school? We need to go back to the basics of humanity. People matter, regardless of their socio economic status, ethnicity, personal choices, or religion. It is not up to you to decide who deserves to be treated nicely or not. You cannot just treat those you like well; you have to extend it to the greater community. This basic standard of kindness has to start at the top of a family unit, with the parents, to have even the faintest hope that it will trickle down to our children. Again—have the same standards for yourself as for your kids.

If you are condescending or impatient to the cashier at your local drive-thru, superior to your house-keeper, impatient towards everyone's children but your own, you can guarantee that this "selective kindness" will be imprinting on your children. We have to model and expect that people deserve to be treated with kindness. Not just if they are nice back, but regardless of whether they deserve it or reciprocate it. That is where confidence comes in—if someone is rude to you after you offer them a spot on the bus or ignores you when you smile at them while waiting in line, oh well. Seriously—oh well! If we decided to be nice based on how other people responded then we would all be doomed.

I made a joke earlier that boys are a mystery to me. Obviously having two girls I feel much more confident to offer insight on this gender, but these standards are for everyone, regardless of gender or age. I have said repeatedly that everyone in the family needs to be held to the same standards in order for these ideas to become authentic and consistent in your home. Remember, these are not new concepts I am throwing at you - these are going back to the beginning. These are basic skills for humanity—definitely not just for children. Because if we want to affect change—real change—that will effect families and become the new standards that are passed down along the generations, then all relationships stand to improve. The goal is to imprint these traits so they become part of who we are, not just how we act.

So as we teach this to our children, both boys and girls, think about when they grow up and get married one day. What kind of a partner do you want for your child? I'd be willing to bet you want a kind, confident and loving person who knows who they are and how to put others ahead of themselves. Who knows how to love and accept love, who is tender and selfless but also has a sense of self so that they can provide security to your child as they grow up and create their own home and have children of their own one day—then become parents who will model these traits and pass them along to your future grandchildren. Now that is a cycle of positivity that I want to be a part of.

So yes, I understand girls more, but I know what kind of a boy I want them to meet one day, and I hope and pray they have been raised with the same qualities so they can be amazing partners to our daughters when they are no longer little girls but wives and mothers themselves. Sniff.

"So God made girls like you make guys like me wanna reach for the brightest star, set it on a ring put it on your hand, grab a piece of land and raise a few more girls like you."
-Kip Moore [22]

MAMA BEAR

♡

MAMA BEAR

....

This is the perfect moment for me to write this chapter. Today started as any other day. Early morning alarm as per usual, quick breakfast and hurried departure to get the girls to school—and then off to my "free time," consisting of a range of meetings, grocery shopping, and various appointments before making it back to school for the last bell of the day. Halfway through my first morning meeting, my cell phone rang. I always get anxious when I see the girls' school number pop up on call display, even though it is usually nothing more than a forgotten bit of homework or a last-minute project that needs to be worked on after school. Today it was the dreaded, "Please come and pick up your daughter, she is sick."

Overall we have been fairly lucky as far as childhood illnesses go. Just a smattering of the usual colds and flus, but nothing too crazy. Today was more of the same; nothing dreadful but there isn't much else that makes your Mama Bear insticts kick in quicker than a sick child.

Walking into the office and seeing my girl waiting quietly with her puffy winter coat and bright orange backpack, her face pale and eyelids heavy instantly made everything else fade a little bit. All those things I had scheduled for the day, all those things I hurriedly had to cancel to come and get my girl, nothing else matters when your child gets sick. And so, I wrapped my arms around her, so small under her layers of school uniform and too-big of jacket, and she snuggled in and murmured, "Hi, Mama." Oh, my heart.

So off we went, heading home for an afternoon of thermometers and popsicles and stuffies. And now she is sleeping beside me—warm and sweaty and lovely—and so I decided to grab my moment and write about being a Mama Bear.

When I first found out that I was pregnant, I was completely overwhelmed with concern about whether or not I was going to be a good mom or even like being a mom at all. Some of you may identify with this and some may not, but I had a lot of friends who were baby crazy and dreamed of the day they would have families of their own. I was not one of these women. Puppies, yes. Babies, no. I was the youngest in my family, didn't have younger cousins that lived nearby, and never really enjoyed babysitting that much. I graduated high school ready for adventure and travel and excitement and though I knew I always wanted to have a family one day, I never felt a rush towards that part of the future. So, in a nutshell,* I wasn't oozing maternal instinct.

These concerns lasted throughout my pregnancy, moderate during the days and spiraling out of control in the nights. But when they handed me my baby girl for the first time—my universe shifted instantly with the most incredible and powerful force I could ever have imagined, and in

* Help, help! I'm in a nutshell!

that moment, I became a Mama Bear.

In the days and weeks and years that followed that miraculous moment, life continued to happen as it does, with good days and bad days, sleepless nights and busy Saturdays, chaos and stress and messy houses and burnt dinners,* and in between all those moments, more joy and laughter than I ever thought possible. As it turns out, the thing I was most afraid of has become my life's greatest blessing. I was put on this earth to be a Mama Bear.

There are many cool things about Mama Bears but my favourite is, of course, how fiercely they protect their cubs. It is an undeniable force of nature. And they go from being just a normal bear, doing their bear thing to being a Mama Bear. One of the most feared forces in the natural world. "Don't come between a Mama Bear and her cubs. You will not live to tell the story." How many times have you heard this warning? My family spent a lot of time outdoors when I was a kid and growing up in the foothills of the Rocky Mountains, you need to be bear aware. We were taught to be cautious of all bears, of course, but extra attention was always spent on warnings about Mama Bears and their cubs.

Another thing that I love about Mama Bears is though they will fiercely protect their cubs, they are super tough on them too. It doesn't take too long for a cub to learn a lesson on respect and boundaries after being a bit too spunky or sassy as they see a whole other side to their big, cozy protective mama. Now I prefer not to toss my children around to teach them a lesson, but you have to respect

* I just burnt a pot of rice right before I sat down to write this chapter. The house still smells terrible.

the line that the Mama Bear has with her cubs. It is not an option to be smug or rude—try it once and the line is drawn in the sand. It is not often a cub will repeat the same mistake twice.

How great would it be if our kids never made the same mistake twice? Wouldn't that take away half of the frustration of parenting? Nothing eats away at a parent's patience quicker than repeated mistakes. That's when the nagging gets involved. The clichéd comments that you swore you would never say to your child. "If I have to ask you one more time…" A real Mama Bear doesn't ask, they just take a big, furry swipe at their cub and that lesson is learned.* Permanently.

I guess my thoughts here are fairly simple. Love your kids fiercely. They need to know that you would do anything for them. You have to be their cheerleader and their support system—it's what a family unit is for. But don't make excuses for them. Don't let them get away with disrespecting you and ignoring you. Don't let them grow up thinking that they are perfect and can do no wrong. That is the quickest recipe for creating a narcissistic adult. Remember the goal here is to raise healthy, successful adults. And that does not come from being told that you can do no wrong. Your kids will do wrong. Many times. And you need to love them fiercely through that. But they also need to learn a healthy fear of consequences and develop an internal desire that makes them not want to disappointment you, or themselves.

* It goes without saying that this behaviour is only acceptable in the animal kingdom, but for legal reasons I want to reiterate this so there are no misunderstandings in this chapter! No swiping of children!

So embrace your inner Mama Bear. Be proud of the love that you have for your children. Protect them to the ends of the earth. Nurture them, guide them, and don't forget to discipline them. This is going to make you actually want to be around them as they get older. Now isn't that a nice thought?

Babies are easy to love. Toddlers are adorably endearing. Primary school kids missing their front teeth—irresistible. Awkward middle schoolers that haven't learned the importance of deodorant ... trickier. Sullen, moody teenagers that suddenly think you are irrelevant ... difficult.

There are going to be times in your parenting journey when you will forget how fiercely you love your kids. And they may forget how much they love you too. They seem to grow up so fast, but in this moment they are small. Try to stop looking at them and thinking, "They are getting so big." Instead remember that in this moment, they are yours. Your child. Whether they are a baby, toddler or teenager—one day you will be looking back on this moment and thinking how young they were. So embrace these moments, embrace your children, and embrace your inner Mama Bear.

SISTER SEPARATION

♡

SISTER SEPARATION

....

I have talked a lot about my girls as individuals throughout this book, but I haven't talked too much about how they are as sisters. There aren't too many relationships in this world that have a more volatile reputation than siblings. Regardless if you have boys or girls or both, I am positive that no parent can claim that they haven't experience some sort of sibling rivalry.

Along with this volatile reputation comes a strange blanket of acceptance. It's just the way kids are. They will appreciate each other when they are older. It's as if parents have given up before they've even started, because it is a basic assumption that sibling rivalry is just something that comes with the territory. And it is to some extent, but that in no way means that it should be treated as an acceptable part of your family.

Yes, I am aware that by writing a book, any book, that shares personal thoughts and opinions on a topic, you open yourself up to criticism. I am sure at some point I may be criticized for being naive and overly optimistic, or unrealistic. That is fine. And it may be true. But I do believe that a little bit of optimism can be the secret ingredient to diffusing a lot of the frustrations we face in our daily lives. So criticize away, but I stand by my position on sibling rivalry. It will happen, that is a given, but that doesn't mean you have to look the other way and dismiss it as a natural part of your children's relationship. As per usual, I won't claim to know too much about the dynamic of boys, but I will confidently share a few thoughts about sisters.

My girls are very close in age and even closer in height. Having the girls so close together made some things harder and some things easier. Sometimes I feel like I have twins but had to have two pregnancies to get them. Not awesome pregnancies either, by the way. And not awesome births. But those are stories I will save for my closest friends. You're welcome.

My first daughter was six months old when I found out I was pregnant with my second. I was as thrilled as I had been rattled with my first pregnancy. My baby girl wasn't crawling yet when I found out she was going to be a big sister, and she decided to celebrate the news by learning to crawl right as my morning sickness kicked in. The months that followed were a bit of a blur, and when my second daughter was born we were suddenly the proud parents of two babies, they were just different sizes. We had two cribs, two different sizes of diapers—two of everything. And the girls don't remember life without each other in it.

So on the easy side—we didn't have to deal with any angst from our first born because she really was too young to have any sort of adjustment. We were already in the zone of diapers and messes and laundry that never ends* and

* Still in that zone.

never, ever having enough sleep. We never had the chance to sleep through the night between kids, so in a weird way it kind of felt like we conquered the need to sleep more than three hours at a time.* The funny thing about sleep is that once you get used to sleeping again after being severely sleep deprived for so long, it actually gets harder and harder to wake up. When the girls were babies, as most mothers would attest to, I would wake at the sound of the slightest snuffle or whimper and go from sleeping soundly to being instantly alert. Now it seems to take both girls literally jumping all over me, or worse,** to wake me up.

On the harder side, well, we were full on in the baby phase and I don't think I finished a sentence to my husband for two years. But the girls have no memories without each other and that is pretty precious.

Now, I know there are a lot of people out there with a lot more kids than I have and closer in age, so I am not trying to say that I had it harder than anyone else—I'm simply sharing some thoughts on those early sibling moments. I can't remember who this tidbit came from, but someone suggested always making your older child ask permission to take a toy from their new sibling—even though the baby wouldn't know or care if a stuffy was being removed from their chubby little fingers— it set a baseline of respect

*Not true—that was merely a coping mechanism our sleep deprivation told us.

* *After seeing *The Parent Trap*[23] for the first time, we had to deal with weeks of pranks from the girls. By far the worst was waking up to one of my girls holding my head back and prying open my mouth while the other one stood above me armed with a can of whipping cream.

that the older child was not the boss. They were a team. So when the silent, motionless little blob suddenly became a loud, busy little blob, there would be an expectation of asking and sharing already established between them.

This is an example of a tiny expectation that sets the foundation for sibling respect as they get older. Your kids won't remember it but somewhere in their subconscious, they will be affected positively by it.

As long as I can remember, I have put my girls in "sister separations" if they are bickering or not getting along. I have a priceless picture of them each standing in their rooms, side by side, peering over two new baby gates that had just been put up in front of each of their rooms. They looked like naughty ponies in a barn. That was one of the many coping mechanisms I used over the years to enforce the dreaded "sister separation," because, ironically, as soon as they were put in it, all they wanted was to be together.

The trick to an effective "sister separation" (sorry moms of boys, all I can think of is "brother break" or "sibling split," both a little lame) is to start them when the bickering is very minor. If they are all-out fighting then a separation is not enough of a punishment. These do not, in any way, replace timeouts, grounding, technology bans, or whatever else you do in your home for discipline. These are specific to your children testing the waters of bickering, not sharing, not deciding on a movie they both want to watch, and any other minor scenario you can think of. Any mild snarkiness between your kids is the perfect chance to pull them away from each other so they can remember that life is actually better and more fun with their sibling in it. That's it.

Make them be bored. Let them stay bored long enough that they are excited to be with their sibling again. Even if it means they have to play Lego when they really wanted to play cars. Whatever the fight was about, we are too quick to solve it with the object they were fighting over, instead of removing the object and each other. Kids don't like to be by themselves with nothing to do. So create this scenario and you have put yourself back at the top of the food chain. Where you are actually supposed to be as a parent.

Another thing I have done with my girls as they have gotten older is make their behaviour toward each other inextricably linked to their friends. What I mean by this is simple: if they aren't treating each other well, they are not allowed to spend time with their friends. It is a hard line in our family. They are each other's first and most important friend. Not by choice but by birth. They can learn to love and embrace this fact and celebrate the friendship they have with each other, or they can miss out on their other friendships. I firmly believe that if they are not treating each other well, they have no right to spend time with other kids.

Over and over I have seen kids spending time with their friends and then their sibling comes around and they are immediately dismissed and treated like a second-class citizen. This is ridiculous, in my opinion*. I'm sorry but family first then friends. If your relationship is not right with your family, you do not deserve to spend time with friends. Simple and effective with the bonus of a much happier home environment.

Integrating something like this into your home is much, much easier with younger children. But it is not impossible to do with older kids. There will be the inevitable

*Please refresh yourself with the * on page 107 in case you disagree with me on this point.

confrontation that most changes bring when you have older children, but if you are confident, consistent, and fair with your integration of this concept then I do believe it will begin to diffuse the rivalry and repair the friendship that your children should and can have with each other.

I never had a sister growing up and but had, and still have, a wonderful friendship with my brother; however, it wasn't until I saw the bond that my girls have with each other that I realized how amazing it would have been to have a sister as well. It really is a privilege and it doesn't do your kids any favours to assume that fighting comes with the territory of being siblings. It is a vicious cycle when children grow up being allowed to treat those closest to them the worst. Don't be afraid to change the rules on this one. Expect and ask for more from your kids. They will thank you for it one day.

TWENTY
SECOND HUGS

♡

TWENTY SECOND HUGS

....

I almost ruined a family vacation once because of a twenty second hug. At the time, I was devastated about the whole episode but now, looking back on it, I actually find it kind of funny. This is huge growth for me because I have always been a people pleaser and put too much pressure on myself to make everything "perfect," especially with my family. It is a funny trait because they don't put this pressure on me; I put it on myself, but it is there, nevertheless. I have such high expectations for things that if there is a blip, I am deeply disappointed and prone to remembering that one particular moment instead of all the good that filled the rest of the experience. This is something I have really had to work on over the years, and in the spirit of self-reflection and transparency I have decided to share this part of myself in this book. I have said repeatedly throughout these chapters that I am not perfect, never claimed to be, and not to expect this of yourself or your kids. So, in that regard, I guess I have to be honest about my downfalls as well. I have a strong love/hate relationship about this particular personality trait because it is a huge part of what makes me put so much effort into whatever I take on, whether it be at work, at home, or planning a family holiday. I am the person who makes the matching t-shirts for vacations, does all the planning with printed out, themed itineraries, and makes the video slide show after we are home. And it all comes from a good place of really wanting everyone to have the best time possible. This is all fine and dandy but it took me a while to realize for myself that this isn't what makes the experience epic—it's the people you share it with. And if there is a blip, that doesn't mean the trip was a bust and it sure shouldn't be the one thing you remember when you get home.

Our families aren't, or shouldn't be, so fragile that one little upset can crack the foundation. A theme throughout this book has been fighting against perfectionism, and I have addressed being cautious with external pressures, such as social media, that can drive you to be a perfectionist, but internal pressure is just as, or more, powerful and needs to be addressed as well. And so, I get to use myself as an example this time—lucky me. But I guess nothing says "authentic" like putting yourself out there as the example instead of just using random scenarios.

So, I started to realize that I had to work on myself in this area when I would think back to a trip or activity and the first thing that came to mind was the fleeting moment that someone hurt someone else's feelings, or I felt like I had been impatient with my kids, or I had forgotten to reserve a car when I said I would. This is not a healthy way to live and something I have been working on. It is so easy to give advice and so hard to apply it to yourself in an authentic way. But I don't think it does anyone any favours to give the illusion that we have it all figured out, and so, in case I have been too subtle about it up until now, I am not perfect. Sorry if this disappoints you. Shoot, now that is all I am going to remember about this writing experience… I disappointed my readers because I am not perfect! Good thing I have been working on myself so I don't care as much as I used to! You are just going to have to get over it. Okay, enough rambling—you are probably wondering what a twenty second hug is and what it has to do with all of this.

So a twenty second hug is scientifically proven[24] to be the magical length that will trigger the release of oxytocin, the "love" hormone, as well as lower levels of stress hormones like cortisol thus creating a calm, peaceful feeling between the two who are embracing—therefore leading to greater happiness and harmony. Not in my opinion, but in the opinion of science. So obviously this is a great thing to bring into our families and parenting methods. For as long as I can remember, I have made our girls "hug it out" and of course those hugs have to last for twenty seconds. It seems like an eternity but when the twenty seconds is over, everything is better*.

The "hug it out" method has been so successful with the sibling relationship in our home that I have naturally brought it into my marriage as well. I often make my husband and I "hug it out," even when one of us just needs a little extra attention, the full twenty-second hug comes out.

Fast forward to the family vacation I almost ruined over this same amazing event that has flooded my home

---

* Except when they lose their balance during the embrace and fall over, bang into each other and hit the floor before bursting into tears, and then everything is worse. Yes, this has happened. More than once.

with love and tenderness. The "event" happened between my husband and my brother. It was over nothing really, something trivial and cliché like a remote.* Like things go with men sometimes, a difference of opinion escalated to the point where I felt an intervention was needed. An intervention in the form of a twenty second hug. Of course it worked perfectly with my two young daughters so why wouldn't it work with two grown men?

You don't have to be a rocket scientist to figure out that this did not go over well and, in fact, aggravated the situation to a far more dire place as I stubbornly insisted on counting out loud to twenty as my six foot three inch husband awkwardly embraced my six foot four inch brother. Yet through it all, I was somehow convinced that if they hung in there until I got to twenty then the situation would magically resolve and peace would be restored. And I wouldn't have to look back at pictures from that summer vacation and remember the upset, I would remember that I swooped in and diffused the situation with my magical twenty second hug.

Unfortunately, life doesn't work this way and I didn't fix everything. But you know what? They figured it out. Without me. And they got over it, and we all went on the have a great summer vacation anyway. And I started my journey of learning that one bad moment doesn't tarnish the rest of the good moments. I also learned that what works with little girls doesn't work with grown men.** And I learned that life goes on and we love each other through

* It was definitely over a remote.

** I know, shocking.

it. Because if I am trying to authentically teach my girls that they do not have to be perfect and I am trying to model that my home and my wardrobe and my Instagram feed doesn't have to be perfect, then I have to allow myself to not be perfect as well. That seems to be the hardest one for me. I can handle the messy house, the ups and downs of parenting, the clothes that wouldn't make the cover of a magazine...yet I still struggle with having the bar too high for my self in my personal relationships. It comes from a place of deep caring and genuinely wanting things to be great for everyone around me but I know that I need to lighten up and remember that in families things go wrong. People make mistakes, say things they don't mean, hurt peoples feelings, apologize and forgive. That is part of being in a family unit with different personalities, different backgrounds and upbringings, different expectations and interests, it is what makes them interesting and unique. Vibrant and full of life and variety. This same diversity is also what can make them complicated but that is okay.

We will all make mistakes at some point but it is not up to you or me to fix or prevent every little blip along the way. Blips happen. Forgiveness happens. Twenty second hugs may or may not happen. Either way, life is good.

NUGGETS OF
WISDOM

♡

NUGGETS OF WISDOM

···

We are given nuggets of wisdom throughout our entire lives. From before we can remember and from a million different sources: family members, neighbours, teachers and friends—from books we read, songs we listen to, and movies we watch, just to name a few. Regardless of whether we remember all of these nuggets or have even asked for them, we receive them and they shape who we are. Simple nuggets, from before our memories allow us to remember, like the importance of sharing and taking turns, saying please and thank you– they live in our subconscious and play a role in our daily lives. More complex nuggets are given as we get older, ones that help us navigate relationships successfully, help us do well in school and later on, our various workplaces. And perhaps the most important nuggets of are saved for advice on marriage and children. Those last topics are, more often than not, our biggest legacies—good or bad.

Before you get married and have children, for me anyway, the wisdom comes and goes but doesn't seem as important as after you become a spouse and a parent.

This is when you really start to realize and acknowledge that in order to survive and to thrive in these new roles, you may need to seek the wise council of those who have gone down these roads before you. It is a classic and normal trait for adolescents and young adults to want to pave their own way, find their own path—to do things their way. It gives them a sense of independence and individuality. All good things. But when these independent individuals suddenly find themselves attached to another human being and with dependents of their own, nuggets of wisdom are suddenly seen in a different light. No longer are they viewed as unsolicited advice; they are now received with gratitude and respect.

In the days leading up to my wedding, I was caught up in the blur of all the showers, fun, and romance that comes before one's wedding day. In the midst of the showers, there were many pieces of advice offered to me as I began to prepare to become a wife. They ranged from practical advice such as "make your bed every morning—it will give your life a sense of order"* to the idealistic "never stop holding hands,"** but the nugget of wisdom I hold dearest to my heart from that stage of my life was from my mom. The night before my wedding she simply told me that if both of us genuinely tried to put each other's need above our own, we couldn't go wrong. So simple, yet so profound. I have thought back to this nugget so many times throughout my marriage—sometimes with a feeling

* I regretfully admit I have not been able to heed this advice. Kind of lame advice at a bridal shower, anyway (sorry to whomever wrote this—it was anonymous).

** Doing much better at this one.

of success and sometimes in disappointment, as the ebb and flow of a marriage will be. But without a doubt, it is the best piece of marital advice I was given, and I believe what makes it so good is its simplicity. We can over think and over explain and over complicate things to a point where we can justify pretty much anything, but I encourage you take it back to the basics and each ask yourself, "Am I putting my partner's needs above my own?" The key word is *each* asking yourself—it doesn't work if only one half of your partnership is unselfish. Otherwise it is a recipe for disaster. Resentment will be inevitable.

I know I am not the first to say that the foundation for a happy family starts with a happy marriage, but I want to go one step further and say it starts with being happy with yourself. If you are married, you can model this unselfish partnership to your children, and they will grow up absorbing these traits as their own little nuggets of wisdom that will help them have healthy relationships of their own one day. When my husband and I were going through premarital counseling, we were encouraged to be proud of our love and not to be afraid to show it off to others. Not in an arrogant way but in a steadfast and confident way that shows those around you, including your children, that your relationship is strong and true. This gives your children a sense of security and belonging in the world.

If you are a single parent, then you have to provide this sense of security and belonging in the world without a partner. You have to show yourself all the same love and respect that you would want for yourself if you were in a relationship. Marital status doesn't give or take the onus off needing to be happy with yourself. You can create this sense of security for your children without a partner if you show them how to be content with themselves by being content with yourself. Teaching your kids to be happy with themselves is an invaluable nugget of wisdom—one that is often taught without words, it is modeled through our actions on a daily basis. And of course, this is a journey—sometimes one of the hardest journeys of our lives—but being aware of its importance is half the battle.

Another nugget of wisdom I received was to never discipline in anger. We are all human and, therefore, all have a breaking point but you need to be aware of when and what your personal breaking point is and to detach it from your discipline. Lay out your consequences prior to this line being crossed so that your kids know what discipline will occur in advance—and then stick to it. This will protect you and your children from a world of regret. And will also model to your children to think before they act, an invaluable lesson as they enter their teenage years.

Another nugget of wisdom I could not have lived without was to keep a sense of humour. I can't count how many times I have disciplined the kids, because it needed to be done, and then gone into my bedroom and laughed about it with my husband. Half the time* we feel like we are playing the role of grown-ups that have a plan and know what we are doing. Most of the time, we are making it up as we go along, chuckling to ourselves along the way.** Don't forget your sense of humour. As much as we have to let our kids make mistakes, we have to let ourselves make mistakes too.

* Or more…

** Mostly behind closed doors so our kids still think we are very mature…

Every new stage that our children go through is a new stage for us too. And for each child too, because they are going to handle every situation different than their siblings. So cut yourself some slack. Dust off your sense of humour. And every once in a while, go behind a closed door and laugh at yourself. Your kids don't have to know you're not really that disappointed with whatever thing they did that warranted the discipline. Sometimes we just have to follow through to make sure our "threats" are taken seriously. At the very least, we have to have an illusion of authority and control! I mentioned before my fondness of the saying, "it takes a village," and there aren't many nuggets of wisdom that trump this one as a parent. Let people in. Let them help you. Make a village for yourself and your family. You are not an island; you do not have to do everything on your own in order to be a successful parent. Family, friends, neighbours, grandparents—we all have a village around us waiting to offer nuggets of wisdom as we wind our way through our various stages of life. Let them in and absorb the wisdom of those around us. You can sift through it and create your own version of the advice you are given, but you don't have to come up with all the answers on your own. Every day is a new day for all of us—parents and children alike—with new challenges, new successes, and new failures. Try not to be too hard on yourself. And don't forget to laugh.

WORDS FOR
YOUR KIDS

♡

WORDS FOR YOUR KIDS

··

When I was a brand-new mom with a squishy, lovely baby girl in my arms, I was full of the wonder and amazement that comes with those early days of motherhood. The world seems to stop after your first child.*The days that blend into nights as you sleep when your baby sleeps,** when you let the laundry pile up without worry because some adoring grandparent will come over and help you with it,*** when you can think of dinner**** with a carefree spirit because you have two months of delicious, homemade

* After your second child, it is chaos—we are talking basic survival skills (I stopped at two, so I can't comment further).

** I could literally cry at the thought that I was once able to nap in the afternoon.

*** Where are they now?! There is way more laundry now! School uniforms, soccer clothes, gymnastics leotards…seriously.

**** Dinner. The word gives me an instant panic attack.

dinners to choose from in the freezer, gifted to you by loving friends and family.

Yes, the early days are bliss.* You are surrounded by a circle of love and support from your family and friends. Even strangers rush to help you with doors and grocery carts and everything else you have to eventually get used to doing on your own. But as the days pass and your babies grow, the things that used to be overwhelming become as second nature as breathing. Those early days do pass quickly though. I heard it perfectly stated once that in the life of a parent "the days are long but the years are short."

So back to my squishy, lovely baby girl. We set off for a playdate** with a former colleague of mine that had recently had her own bundle of joy.

As the morning progressed, I was asked a question that began a conversation I thought about for years to come: "What words have you chosen for your child that you want them to embody as they grow up?" Yikes. I thought I was just coming over for coffee. I hadn't thought of any words of meaning for my baby girl and was suddenly put on the spot in a way that was going to reflect what kind of a mother I was not only in that moment but for all the years to come! I panicked for more reasons than one, but mostly because my intelligence had been seriously reduced since the birth of my child, and I had recently been thinking and communicating through a series of monosyllabic grunts. I managed a fairly subtle deflection and got her to answer

* Other than the obvious. Cringe.

** Playdate = placing two immobile, adorable blobs of chub on the floor beside each other.

her own question first, which turned out to be a mistake because the thought and intention to which she answered put even more pressure on my own answer.

I don't remember exactly what she said, but I know it was good. She talked about character traits like leadership skills, intelligence, confidence, tenacity, strength, and vision for her future. All good things for sure. I kind of felt like I saw her baby turning into a tiny adult right in front of my eyes as she was speaking. So when she turned expectantly to me and I knew it was my turn, I answered quickly but was suddenly very sure of myself: "I want her to be kind." Honestly, my friend looked a bit disappointed and politely waited for me to elaborate.

I went on to justify my answer by comparing my trait with hers. The words that she chose for her child were wonderful—please don't misunderstand this, and they are good things to hope for your kids—but they are B-level traits. Kindness is an A-level trait because it is the foundation for all the other stuff to be built on top of. If you put all your energy into raising your child to be a strong leader, but forget to instill kindness in them—you will create a ruler that doesn't care for those underneath them—as we looked at in Leaderschmuck. If you invest all of your energy into honing your child's intelligence, your child may end up being really smart, but what if they don't? What if you have a child with a learning disability or who struggles in school but has a passion for the arts or the outdoors in a way that doesn't fulfill your dream for their academic intelligence? Then you have a child that feels like they disappointed you. Or what if your efforts do give you the results of a successful academic? They may end up superior and smug if they don't have this rooted in kindness or may feel their worth is tied to their grades, as we talked about in Confagance. We explored what happens when you raise a child to be confident without kindness and the arrogance that can take over your child's personality and effect how they treat others. Tenacity, strength, and vision - awesome traits to have but without being rooted in kindness, to what lengths will they go to get what they want? This is when people will justify hurting others to reach their own goals.

But when you wish kindness upon your child, and then learn who they are as they grow, they will teach you what their B-level skills and gifts are. And they will have the balance to know that what they do doesn't make them who they are. And they will treat others with respect and dignity along the way.

I wouldn't change my answer, and I truly feel that kindness is the most undervalued of all human traits. If we could breathe this back into our children and ourselves, it would make such a difference in our homes, schools, and society as a whole. I painted a picture to hang above our mantel a few years ago. It simply says, "BE KIND" in large, bold letters with the corresponding Eph 4:32 in small print in the bottom right hand corner.* I intentionally made the Bible verse the subtle part of the painting because, remember, you do not have to be a Christian to be kind. This is a human quality we are talking about, not a spiritual one—which

* It actually says Esph 4:32 because I spelled the abbreviation for Ephesians wrong, which my father-in-law pointed out as soon as he saw it hanging up the first time. I told him that if he read the first part of the sign, he would have known it wasn't very kind to have pointed out my mistake right away. Actually that wasn't super kind of me either, so the whole conversation completely failed the point of the sign.

WORDS FOR YOUR KIDS

we discussed in more detail in Religapointment—so if you are skimming this book in Chapters, flipped to the end and are now wondering if you should buy it, don't worry, it isn't blasphemous.

So the point of this isn't that it is bad to have words for your kids, and have hopes and dreams for them. Just the opposite, in fact—choose words to breath into their lives and have dreams for them so they will grow up learning to live with passion and intention. But don't choose their life for them. Don't worry about how smart or successful they will be. That is not what makes them valuable and precious and unique. Don't teach them that success is measured through achievement. Teach them to live well, to dream big and instill in them a zest for life filled with kindness and love and passion.

Cinderella[25] recently recaptured the world's imagination with the remake of the classic cartoon a few years back. Though the movie is obviously a fairy tale, there was more truth spoken in that film than most of the movies that I have seen.

The dying mother's final words of wisdom to her child as she prepared to leave her daughter alone in the world were:

"Have courage, and be kind."

Thank you, Cinderella. That is a reminder we all needed. So, have courage and be kind. And teach your children how to do this too. Model it for them and let them grow up in a world where this isn't the exception, it is the expectation. So they go on to become healthy parents themselves and then can raise another generation of youth that embody these traits. And so on and so on. Maybe if we can embrace this simple truth and stop worrying about all the stuff that doesn't matter, we can start to restore our world to a place where people begin to remember what *really* matters. Don't get caught up in the small stuff. When you look back on your life, you aren't going to remember the sleepless nights, the report cards, how nice your lawn looked, the clothes you wore or the car you drove. You are going to remember your family, how you treated people, and how you raised your kids. And whether they are happy, kind, successful, and well-adjusted adults in healthy relationships of their own. And you're going to remember family vacations. You are definitely going to remember family vacations … I think I need to book another one soon. YOLO.

♡

AFTERWORD

···

You can now order
"Congragegagement ™ Cards"
on my website www.kindfident.com

I told you I would trademark it.

♡

ACKNOWLEDGMENTS

···

Like I said in the Introclaimer, I have never had great aspirations to be a writer, but once my family knew about this book, they were incredibly supportive. Except for my kids. They just made fun of me. But for the most part, I felt very affirmed. The biggest thanks has to go to my parents who deserve a huge shout-out for the crazy love they have for me. I have never doubted my place in this world for a second because of them. And for my husband who has the most teachable spirit of anyone that I know. He is the definition of a best friend, and I love that we still laugh until we cry together. And my girls. My sweet girls—I never knew love could run so deep until I had them. They bring me pure joy.

So that's it then. I wrote a book—a real book. Not something I ever thought I would do, but it sure was fun. Thank you for noticing it on the shelf and taking a chance on it. I hope you enjoyed it even half as much as I enjoyed writing it.

With love and thanks,

Shayla ♡

♡

NOTES

....

1.   Try *Mother Teresa: A Life of Kindness* by Ellen Weiss, available for order on amazon.com—much better advice than mine, I'm sure.

2.   Sophie Kinsella's Shopaholic series is ridiculously funny and easy to read. The movie is fun too. If you don't laugh out loud at this book, you have a problem.

3.   *Mean Girls*, 2004 · Teen film/comedy, starring Lindsay Lohan. Now you know why I apologized.

4.   *Bringing Up Boys* by Dr. James Dobson, available for order on www.drjamesdobson.org. Not sure what else to tell you about that—I obviously have not read it.

5.   Phil Dunphy … *Modern Family* … if you don't watch it we can't be friends.

6.   "Narcissistic Personality Disorder." Psychology Today. Accessed April 17, 2017. https://www.psychologytoday.com/us/conditions/narcissistic-personality-disorder.

7.   *Wonder* by R.J. Palacio, available to order on amazon.com or at pretty much any other bookstore in the world. Just go buy it.

8.   *Auggie & Me.* See above. Ditto.

9.   Giordano, Suzy, and Lisa Abidin. *The Baby Sleep Solution: A Proven Program to Teach your Baby to Sleep Twelve Hours a Night.* New York: Perigree Books, 2006.

10.   Leman, Kevin. *Have a New Kid by Friday.* Fleming H. Revell Company, 2008.

11.   Attachment Parenting: Co-sleeping and breastfeeding for a really, really, really long time.

12.   Authoritarian Parenting: Most of our grandparents. "Do as I say, not as I Do" types.

13.   Holistic Parenting: You use a lot of aromatherapy and are probably a vegan.

14.   Permissive Parenting: See chapter 3 for the definition of Waschlappen. Pretty much letting your kids do whatever.

15.   Positive Parenting: Smiling while you try not to yell at your kids but deep down you really, really want to.

16.   Helicopter Parenting: If you bubble wrap your kids before you take them to the park, this is you. Or if you don't take them to the park at all, because it is too dangerous.

17.   Free Range Parenting: Letting your kids be in control of their schedule and development. Basically, you let them go to bed whenever they want to avoid the "bedtime battle" and hope they eventually get so tired they decide they want to go to bed at a normal time.

18.   Dolphin Parenting: A balance of all the above in one big happy family—er, pod.

19.   Ikaria, Greece—an island in the Aegean Sea, 10 nautical miles southwest of Samos. Population: 8,432. Until I move there anyway.

20.   *Desiderata.* 1927 poem by American writer Max Ehrmann. (Latin for "desired things").

21.   Dean Brody—"8th Day," from the *Beautiful Freakshow* album (2016).

22.   Kip Moore—"More Girls Like You," from the *Slowheart* album (2017).

23.   *The Parent Trap*—the 1961 original and the 1998 remake are chock-full of great prank ideas. You've been warned.

24.   Scientifically proven by Dr. Mercola (I think).

25.   *Cinderella*, Disney Film, 2015—just watch it; it is so good.

CPSIA information can be obtained
at www.ICGtesting.com
Printed in the USA
LVHW092240040319
609506LV00005B/24/P